Journeys of a Spiritual Activist

by Raheel Raza

Sacred Activism is the fusion of the mystic's passion for God with the activist's passion for justice.

—Andrew Harvey

Other titles in by **Possibly Publishing**:

Journeys
of a
Spiritual Activist

First Edition

by

Raheel Raza

Journeys of a Spiritual Activist
by Raheel Raza

Afterword by Ya'qub ibn Yusuf

Edited by Clinton Joe Andersen, Jr.

Copyright © 2017 by Raheel Raza
Copyright © 2017 by Ya'qub ibn Yusuf

Raheel Raza retains all rights to publish and republish in any other format all of her works presented in this book.

Ya'qub ibn Yusuf retains all rights to publish and republish in any other format all of his works presented in this book.

Possibly Publishing
www.possiblypublishing.com

All rights reserved. No part of this book may be reproduced or transmitted in any form or by any means, electronic or mechanical, including but not limited to photocopying, recording or by any information storage and retrieval system, without written permission from the author, except for the inclusion of brief quotations for critical reviews.

ISBN-10: 0-9819437-7-2
ISBN-13: 978-0-9819437-7-0

First Printing of this "First Edition": December 2017
Digital publication date 12/31/2017 7:36 PM from <The Spiritual Activist Rev 2.1.doc>

1 3 5 7 9 10 8 6 4 2

Design & Composition: Possibly Publishing
Cover design: Possibly Publishing
Cover Art: Adnan Syed of Adcom

This book is dedicated to my fellow activists who are struggling to reclaim the beauty of our faith.

Journeys of a Spiritual Activist

CONTENTS

Preface 1

The Urgency of Islam's Spiritual Message 3

Female Spirituality in Islam 11

The Parliament of World Religions 17

Stepping Stones on My Journey 23

Rumifest Rocked 27

The Masks of God 29

Epiphany Explorations 31

Have Yourself a Merry Muslim Christmas 33

The Spirit of Ramzan 35

Diversity, Transformation and Hope 39

All This Singing, Just One Song 45

The Muslim New Year: A Time for Reflection 49

Letter to My Best Friend 53

In Memoriam for My Father 61

No Compulsion Here... Yet! 65

From Darkness to Light 69

A Birthday Reborn 73

CONTENTS *(Continued)*

The Ultimate Journey to the Center of Our Faiths 77
Women of Faith Build Hope and Homes 89
Finding Spirituality in India 95
Searching for The Divine 103
Bearing Witness to Truth and Reconciliation 107
From Su-Shi to Su-Fi: A Unique Eid Celebration 111
The Colors of Autumn Merge: with the Color of Islam 113
Officiating a Marriage is Alright and a Woman's Right 115
Helena's Voyage and Paul's Journey 119
Spirit of the East: A Sacred Music Concert 123
Finding Peace in Kincardine 127
Journeys to the Center of My Soul 129
The Call of Rumi—from Konya 131
Operation One Heart at a Time 135

AFTERWORD by Ya'qub ibn Yusuf 141

   About Raheel Raza 161

Preface

People often ask me how I could do the work I do in activism and also be spiritual. Somehow it seems to them that the two are at odds with each other. For me they are not, as I grew up with rituals but embraced spirituality and that has been my path ever since.

In the early years, right after 9/11 when I started speaking out about the virus of extremism within our midst, I found the work very toxic. It left me exhausted and bereft of positive energy. I used to pray for a balm on my soul.

Then one day many years ago, I came across the Sufis and was immediately hooked to their beautiful philosophy. Simultaneously I experienced other forms of spirituality within many other faiths and cultures and I was automatically attracted to them.

I also discovered that in the journey of life, nothing is a coincidence. When we open our hearts to mysticism and spirituality, amazing doors open for us. This is what happened to me. I found myself being invited, drawn to people and places soaked in spirituality and I let the flow take me over. Some of the experiences were magical, others mystical beyond words

In the Qur'an God asks us "do you not see the signs of God?" This is what I started to note. My senses became more attuned to the beauty that surrounds us and I found the balm to my soul that I prayed for.

I started making notes of my experiences because some of them were too profound to explain. This book is about that journey of my life towards the centre of my soul. The journey has not ended yet.

I am open and eager to embrace what is to come.

Raheel Raza
Toronto, Canada
2017

The Urgency of Islam's Spiritual Message

> *A life is either all spiritual or not spiritual at all. No man can serve two masters. Your life is shaped by the end you live for. You are made in the image of what you desire.*
>
> *Thomas Merton*

Faith is not politics, and politics is not faith. And this is the critical difference between political Islam and the spiritual message of my faith.

Islam at its core is the affirmation of belief in One God. Islam's holy text the Quran repeatedly reminds Muslims and others who may read the text—that Islam is not a new religion but the elemental faith of man, the belief and witness to the reality of One God as the source and origin of all things in the universe. This primal faith gets repeatedly corrupted, yet God sends prophets and messengers to reform the corrupted faith and remind people how their sorrow in this world is a product of their corruption born as they deliberately or mistakenly, wander away from the path prescribed.

Dr. Karen Armstrong, a theologian who has written extensively about faith speaks to this conundrum in faith.

She says that each faith tradition represents a constant dialogue between a timeless, transcendent, or sacred reality and the constantly changing circumstances of life here on earth. We all have to struggle to make our scriptures and the insights of our tradition speak to the circumstances we find ourselves in.

Islam is a reminder to each and every soul endowed with free will of its connection with God, of its responsibility and accountability on the Day of Reckoning, of the relationship of God and man in the divine scheme of things. Those who acknowledge this cosmological reality and submit to it, living out of obedience, faith, love, devotion—however one wants to explain the meaning of submission which is one of the meanings of the word "Islam" in Arabic, that person is then at peace within, while the outward reality of such person would reflect God's mercy and compassion. Professor Salim Mansur explains eloquently

> The outward turmoil in an individual or a nation is the absence of spirituality, inner peace and harmony, and nothing better reveals the wisdom of this message then the present state of Muslims and their nations so utterly in disrepair indicating how greatly absent is God's spiritual message as delivered to Muhammad, from their lives."

As for Muhammad, he is best described and understood thru the lens of the non-Muslim scholar, Rev. Bosworth Smith, in *Mohammed and Mohammadanism* writes

> He was Caesar and Pope in one; but he was Pope without Pope's pretensions, Caesar without the legions of Caesar: without a standing army, without a bodyguard, without a palace, without a fixed revenue; if ever any man had the right to say that he ruled by the right divine, it was Mohammed, for he had all the power without its instruments and without its supports.

But don't take my word for this. There is a current biography of Mohammad—one of the best I have read called The First Muslim by Lesley Hazelton who is a secular Jew and calls herself an accidental theologian.

At age 40 Muhammad had a profound spiritual experience when he was visited by the angel Gabriel and it was his spirituality that inspired those around him.

When the Quran was revealed as a message to Mohammad, he was living in a society that was pluralistic so the Quran addresses diversity calling it a blessing from the creator. The Quran, a word that means "The Reading" is not just a book of laws but is more of a moral and ethical guide with some beautifully spiritual and uplifting passages if only we would comprehend.

God is the light of the heavens and the earth.
The smile of God's light is like a niche in which is a lamp,
the lamp in a globe of glass,
the globe of glass as if it were a shining star,
lit from a blessed olive tree
neither of the East nor of the West,
its light nearly luminous
even if fire did not touch it.
Light upon light!

The Qur'an (24:35)
al 'nuur—the light

The Quran also clearly elucidates that this is not a stand-alone message but has to be practiced in conjunction with the teachings of the messages that came before i.e. Judaism and Christianity being closest as Abrahamic faiths.

The striking fact on first reading of the Quran is how much of its message is Jewish and Christian. The Quran tells the story of Jews, of Abraham and Moses, of Jesus and Mary among others.

There is an entire chapter titled Maryam or Mary which tells the story of the virgin birth.

It's also remarkable how Muslims, despite their daily readings of the Quran, tend to obscure this fact that we send blessings on the progeny of Abraham five times a day in our daily prayers.

If Muslims were to sincerely and truly follow the spiritual message of Islam, they would understand how much Jesus is revered and perhaps the persecution of Christians in Muslim lands would cease. In chapter *An-Nisa* verse 171 we read

> Indeed, the Messiah Jesus the son of Mary is the Messenger of God, His Word revealed on Mary, and a spirit sent from Him.

Jesus, or Isa in Arabic, is deemed by Islam to be a prophet. He is referred to by name in 25 different verses of the Quran and six times with the title of "Messiah" (or "Christ", depending on which Quranic translation is being used). He is also referred to as the "Messenger" and the "Prophet" but, perhaps above all else, as the "Word" and the "Spirit" of God. No other prophet in the Quran, not even Muhammad, is given this particular honour. In fact, among the 124,000 prophets said to be recognized by Islam—a figure that includes all of the Jewish prophets of the Old Testament—Jesus is considered second only to Muhammad, and is believed to be the precursor to the Prophet of Islam.

In his fascinating book The Muslim Jesus, the former Cambridge professor of Arabic and Islamic studies Tarif Khalidi brings together, from a vast range of sources, 303 stories, sayings and traditions of Jesus that can be found in Muslim literature, from the earliest centuries of Islamic history. These paint a picture of Christ not dissimilar to the Christ of the Gospels. The Muslim Jesus is the patron saint of asceticism, the lord of nature, a miracle worker, a healer, a moral, spiritual and social role model.

According to Islamic theology, Christ did not bring a new revealed law, or reform an earlier law, but introduced a new path or way (*tariqah*) based on the love of God; it is perhaps for this reason that he has been adopted by the mystics, or Sufis, of Islam.

Briefly Sufism is a movement arose from within Islam in the 8th-9th centuries C.E. as an ascetic movement. Its followers seek to find divine truth and love through direct encounters with God. Sufism developed religious practices focusing on strict self control that enable both psychological and mystical insights as well as a loss of self, with the ultimate goal of mystical union with God. Sufism's philosophical principles and ritual practices include writing and reciting poetry and hymns; some of the most famous and beautiful literature of the Islamic world has been written by Sufis.

The Sufi philosopher al-Ghazali described Jesus as "the prophet of the soul" and the Sufi master Ibn Arabi called him "the seal of saints". The Jesus of Islamic Sufism, as Khalidi notes, is a figure "not easily distinguished" from the Jesus of the Gospels.

I also want to focus on the term Jihad which has become the most abused and misused Islamic concepts, because there is a spiritual component to this term as well. Ziauddin Sardar a British academic and author writes ""Constant struggle for justice manifests itself as Jihad. It means 'directed struggle' and can take a number of forms. A tradition of the Prophet declares that "the supreme jihad is against oneself": that is, against one's ego, greed and insatiable desires. Jihad could also, for example, be aimed at the social development of a community. It can also be intellectual—directed against oppressive and totalitarian thought or towards the intellectual uplifting of a society. Lastly, jihad can also take the form of physical struggle against oppression and aggression. Jihad is thus more than simply 'holy war.' But jihad cannot be a war of aggression, or a war for territorial gain, or to impose a particular political order on people. It is a defensive war which places certain responsibilities on those who are called to engage in it. As a moral exercise, jihad must be performed strictly under the Islamic rules of engagement. This means that innocent individuals, women, children and unarmed civilians cannot be harmed, property, and places of worship of other faiths cannot be demolished. As such, kidnapping, hostage-taking, suicide bombings, indiscriminate shooting of civilians, placing bombs in areas and buildings where people work, are evil deeds that Islam totally condemns."

Kabir Helminski a practicing Sufi mystic and author asks a question that is on the lips of many people. "As one scans the Muslim world today for signs of intellectual and spiritual engagement, where are the signs of life? At a time when the world is experiencing an explosion of knowledge and is facing unprecedented challenges on a global scale, who in the Muslim world can offer intellectual or spiritual leadership? Where is Islamic intellectual and spiritual leadership in the face of the ecological catastrophe, disarmament, human rights? Where is the artistic and cultural contribution of contemporary Islamic artists? If Rumi, one of the greatest Sufis can be one of the most popular authors in America, where are the Rumis of today?"

Today many Muslims have sidelined the spiritual message of Islam, the connections to the Abrahamic faith and have turned Islam into a political ideology that is exclusionary and violent. Instead of educating masses about the historical heritage of the faith, there is a dire need to blame someone for all the ills facing humanity. In my recent trips to many Muslims countries, I've been appalled to hear blame being mounted upon the Jewish people, Israel & neo-cons for everything from the Tsunami to controlling the worlds finances and media. They thrive on conspiracy theories because this helps them deflect the real issues facing us.

We have allowed the extremists voices to run rampant. But there are solutions.

Many Muslims today, see the spiritual tradition as the potential answer to the extremism that has hijacked the faith and misrepresented it to the world.

Seyyed Hossein Nasr, professor of Islamic studies at George Washington University in Washington, D.C. says the influence of Sufism can be immense.

"In the Islamic world, Sufism is the most powerful antidote to the religious radicalism called fundamentalism as well as the most important source for responding to the challenges posed by modernism," Nasr adds. "Sufism has kept alive the inner quality of ethics and spiritual virtues, rather than a rigid morality ... and it provides access to knowledge of the divine reality," which affects all other aspects of one's life.

But Sufi practice faces intense pressures in Islam's internal struggle. Dr. Akbar Ahmed, a renowned anthropologist who teaches at American University in Washington says "What the Western world is not seeing is that there are three distinct models in play in the Muslim world: modernism, which reflects globalization, materialism, and a consumer society; the literalists, who are reacting, sometimes violently, against the West and globalization; and the Sufis, who reject the search for power and wealth in favor of a more spiritual path."

But can Sufism influence or counter the political rise of the radicals? Puritanical reformers call Sufis heretics. And modernizers have often denigrated them. Kemal Ataturk, the founder of modern secular Turkey, for instance, closed down the Sufi orders, including

Rumi's Mevlevi order. But the beauty of a genuine spiritual message is that it can't be contained or silenced.

"Some of the greatest reform movements in the 19th century were carried out by Sufis," says Nasr. "Amir Abd al-Kader, the national hero of Algeria, was a Sufi master."

No reliable statistics exist for numbers of Sufis practicing today, as both Sunni and Shiite Muslims may also be Sufis. But many Sufi orders, in which serious students follow a master teacher, have become international in scope. (In the US, Sufi movements vary considerably, and a few have taken on New Age elements and are not directly related to Islam.)

The strategically right thing to do is provide moral and material assistance to Muslims struggling against Islamists. The emphasis of the West in defeating political Islam must be the same as applied towards defeating communism.

Female Spirituality in Islam

> *I shall not lose sight of the labor of any of you who labors in My way, be it man or woman; each of you is equal to the other)*
> *The Koran (3:195)*

Spiritual equality, responsibility and accountability for both men and women is a well-developed theme in the Quran. Whatever the Koran says about the relationship between God and the individual is not in gender terms. With regards to spirituality there are no rights of women distinct from rights of men.

This is well reflected in the verse of the Koran: 33:35

And men who surrender to Allah,
And women who surrender
And men who believe, And women who believe
And men who speak the truth,
And women who speak the truth
And men who persevere in righteousness,
And women who persevere
And men who are humble,
And women who are humble
And men who give alms,
And women who give alms
And men who fast, and women who fast
And men who guard their modesty,
And women who guard their modesty
And men who remember Allah much,
And women who remember Allah much
Allah hath prepared for them forgiveness
and a vast reward.

These verses not only bring out the spiritual equality of the believers, men and women, but also describe most exquisitely those spiritual virtues whose cultivation is necessary for attaining the greatest spiritual reward. It's important to note that In Islam the union with the Divine is contingent upon love of the Prophet.

Since, in their union with the Divine, distinctions are not made among the lovers of God, it follows that no distinction can be made between Muslim men and women in their capacity and longing to reach the Divine.

Several works on women in Islamic History mention distinguished women saints outstanding in their spiritual character—sapiential knowledge, perfection, wisdom, graciousness and magnanimity—but the light of the hidden jewel of the inner personality of hundreds of women saints whose shrines are found all over the Islamic world, has not shone on the pages of Islamic history as we read it.

The title of saint was bestowed upon women equally with men, and since Islam has no order of priesthood and no priestly caste, there was nothing to prevent a woman from reading the highest religious rank in the hierarchy of Muslim saints. From the first days of Islam, there is Khadija, the Prophet's wife also known as umm ul momineen, mother of believers who spiritual strength supported the Prophet in his mission. Some theologians name Fatema, the Prophets daughter as the first "qutb" or spiritual head of the Sufi fellowship. Below the qutb were 4 "awtad" and next in rank were 40 'abdal' or substitutes who are described as being the pivot of the foundation and support of the affairs of men. Jami relates how someone was asked "How many are the Abdal?" and he answered "40 souls". When someone asked him why he didn't say "40 men?" he replied "There have been women among them".

So, from the earliest days of Islam where pious women were blessed with the company of the Prophet and led a spiritual life under his guidance (sahabiyyat) to the spiritual life of great female saints, female spirituality has adorned every century of Islamic history. A considerable number of women of the ninth and tenth centuries are mentioned in the Arabic and Persian sources for their extraordinary achievements in piety and mysticism as well as being traditionalists, poets or calligraphers. There is a feminine dimension of Islamic spirituality reflected in the doctrines concerning the nature of God, the wedding of the soul and spirit. Forms of women manifest gentleness and the serene receptivity of the soul at peace with God. In them Gods own beauty reveals itself clearly as the image of the divine beloved. The outward form of the world is not important.

Female spirituality is manifest in those women who follows a spiritual path and are guided by their love for God, which they express according to the Koranic revelation. Their adornment consists in the remembrance of God, and thru spiritual discipline they cultivate virtues of patience, piety, humility, charity, truthfulness, and absolute dependence on God's will (tawakkul)—the beautiful truth is that God is ever close to those men and women who seek Him.

In the world of mysticism, a human being's meaning or reality is his spirit while his body or outward form is the prison from which he must escape. However one cannot function without the other. So it is said" when a woman walks in the way of God like a man, she cannot be called a woman."

According to the spiritual teachings of Maulana Jelaluddin Rumi: "She is the radiance of God, she is not your beloved. She is the creator—you could say that she is not created". Rumi also said: "in view of the intellect, heaven is the man, and earth the woman—whatever one throws down, the other nurtures"

The Sufis loved to tell stories about female saints and spiritual women, so much of the history of female spirituality is told in folklore. There is a touching legend of Lalla Mimunah in the Maghreb. She was a poor black slave who asked the captain of a boat to teach her the ritual prayer, but she could not remember the formula correctly. To learn it once more, she ran behind the departing boat—walking on the water.. Her only prayer was: "Mimunah knows God and God knows Mimunah". She became a saint greatly venerated in North Africa.

Later in history, the feminine gender was used in many mystical odes as symbols of divine beauty and perfection.

Islamic mysticism or Sufism, more than the stern orthodoxy of traditional Islam, offered women a certain amount of possibilities to participate actively in the religious and social life. In the later Middle Ages, the chronicles tell about convents where women could gather in pursuit of the mystical path or religious life in general. In Mamluk Egypt, these convents had a Shaykha who led the congregation in service and prayer.

While male mysticism and Sufism is an established norm, the role of women sponsoring sufi activities should also be outlined. It was in this field that pious wealthy women found an outlet for their energies and could do much good by offering facilities for dervish gatherings. They found spiritual rewards in gathering of the mystics. Many of these women went on to become revered saints. Anatolia can boast of a large number of small shrines where historical women are buried—noble and simple village women whose very names suggest sad stories. The same is true in Iran but the area where women saints flourished most is probably Muslim India.

Histories of the lives of saints frequently reveal that their mothers played a vital role in leading them towards the spiritual path. To cite an example, Sultan Bahu who is renowned for his spirituality, often mentioned his mother with the utmost reverence and firmly believed that his spiritual attainment was solely due to the efforts of his mother, who was a deeply spiritual woman.

The fact that the first true Saint of Islam was a woman—the great lover Rabia al Adawiyya has helped shape the image of the ideal pious women who can be praised in glowing terms. Rabia has been included in the rank of saints and mystics, because God does not regard outward forms. The root of the matter is not form, but intention.

Rabia was born in a mud hut to a poor family in Basra so she is also called Rabia al Basri. Rabia became a model of selfless love and introduced the concept of love of God in the somewhat austere teachings of her ascetic predecessors, addressing her yearning for Allah in beautiful verses. She lived a simple life in poverty, but her hut served as a treasure house of spiritual wisdom, Blessings and Gods' mercy.

This is well reflected in the allegorical story of when a robber came to her hut and found nothing but pitcher of water. As he was about to leave, Rabia said to him "if you are really a thief then do not leave without taking anything". The thief replied sarcastically "What is there to be taken?" Rabia replied "O needy one, perform the ablution with the water in the pitcher, enter the prayer room and say two rakats of prayer. Then leave after receiving something". The thief obeyed and when he stood for prayer, Rabia also prayed to the Almighty, "O Lord, this man has found nothing here. I have brought him to Thy door, bless him by Thy bounty and Grace." In response to Rabias appeal to the Hearer of Prayers, the thief felt spiritual absorption and joy and continued his prayers. Early in the morning when Rabia entered the prayer room, she found him prostrate before the almighty seeking repentance.

It is said of Rabia:

If all women were like as the one we have mentioned
Then women would be preferred to men
For the feminine gender is no shame for the sun
Nor is the masculine gender an honour
for the crescent moon.

Finally, for those who criticize the injunctions of the shariah concerning women and the role of women in general in Islam (which I will address later today in detail). Such people do not understand the rights bestowed upon women in Islam. The Prophet conferred on women a dignified status commensurable with their feminine role and responsibilities. Most important of all, the vistas of spiritual growth and development were fully opened to the female sex. As a result, in the context of Islamic spirituality, once a woman strives in the spiritual life, she is able to gain access to all the possibilities of the Islamic tradition and to become, like a man, the vicegerent of God (Khalifat Allah) on earth.

The Parliament of World Religions

> *There will be no peace among nations without peace among the religious.*
>
> **Hans Kung**

I had just finished performing my Jum'a namaz (Friday prayers) on the shores of the Mediterranean sea and as I looked around me, I was filled with the wonder of being here—a long way from my native Pakistan and my adopted home, Canada.

I was in Barcelona to attend the 4th Parliament of World Religions with two friends and partners in interfaith—Reverend Dr. Karen Hamilton, a practicing Christian, and Barbara Siddiqui, born in Midland as a Christian and now a practicing Muslim.

It was an unusual situation in many ways. Two white women wearing shalwar qameez were praying with me and a host of diverse Muslims, in a VIP tent set up by the Sikh community of Birmingham, England. We were joined by local media keen to see how Muslims pray. (Thank God men and women prayed together!) However they were thoroughly confused when a turbaned Sikh and some non-Muslims came and joined the prayer. However this was interfaith at it's best. The ad-hoc Imam said in his sermon "Humanity is one Community" and certainly at this point in time, anyone would agree.

The 2004 Parliament of World Religions was organized in partnership with the Universal Forum of Cultures—Barcelona 2004 (which runs from May to September) and in association with the UNESCO Centre of Catalonia. 8000 Religious and spiritual practitioners from all over the world converged to Barcelona to greet and meet each other in peace. 400 carefully selected seminars, workshops, performances and films were offered in the PWR program. They addressed three core themes: Sustainable development, Cultural diversity and Conditions for peace through spiritual practice, religious identity, and intra- and inter-religious dialogue. The Forum was supported by the presence of people like The Archbishop of Barcelona, Dr. Abdullah Omar Nasseef (President of the Muslim World Congress), Ela Gandhi (granddaughter of Mahatama Gandhi), Rabbi Henry J. Sobel (Chief Rabbi of Brazil) and many more.

What was I doing there? I've been dabbling in interfaith dialogue since I moved to Canada in 1989, but September 11th threw me into the heart of interfaith dialogue. Last year, I saw a call for papers for PWR and I immediately called my partners in interfaith dialogue, Karen and Barbara and said, "I'm going—are you coming with me?" They were thrilled at the opportunity. Of course the fact that the venue is Barcelona only added to our desire to be there. We worked together on a proposal titled "Keeping the Path Clear— Women engaging in Inter-faith, Inter-action and Inter-relationships". By June 2004 we hadn't heard back from PWR but we decided to go anyway. At the end of June, I was looking through the online program and I found our names—our proposal had been accepted!

For me, this was a journey from the heart. Whenever I read or talked about Muslim history, I used to imagine the rich Muslim, Jewish and Christian heritage of Spain when the three faiths lived in harmony and reached out to each other spiritually and intellectually. Here was a chance to promote that same essence of pluralism and I felt specially blessed to be chosen for this opportunity. It was only later I discovered how fortunate we were to be chosen from among the thousands of proposals that were submitted.

On our first day in Barcelona, Barb, Karen and I took the Metro to the Forum site. On the metro we met a South Asian couple wearing PWR badges and we chatted. As we exchanged names the lady said "so you are Raheel Raza?" I was a bit shocked. She was the Vice President of PWR and she knew me through our proposal, which she said she personally approved because there weren't too many Muslim women presenters from North America. We were thrilled and humbled at the same time—to be invited to present along with theologians like Hans Kung, Nobel Peace Prize Laureate Adolfor

Perez Esquivel (the Portuguese writer), activists like Susan George and authors like Deepak Chopra—it was a gift.

The Forum site is a 30-hectare space next to the Mediterranean Sea and an extension of the waterfront that began with the 1992 Olympic Games. It was a sight for sore eyes and hearts. A sea of people in colors of the world. Dresses, voices, faces of diversity. The orange robes of Buddhist monks mingling with white dresses of the Sufis—everyone stopped and wished each other in peace, smiled and sometimes spontaneously hugged each other. This was beyond tolerance—it was embracing each other.

Throughout the Forum site there were 4 major exhibitions, 22 smaller shows, 400 concerts, 170 music groups, 60 street performances and 4 circuses. No matter where you went, there were interactive installations, markets, games and fun. Two permanent were remarkable: Voices and Corners Make Cities (photos). The event was hi-tech and well organized with hundreds of youth volunteers from all over the world.

Our trio caused some surprise—a yogi nun from America who had heard Shirin Ebadi speak at the plenary told me she had never met such strong Muslim women before and she hoped we would change the world!

Shirin Ebadi, Nobel Peace Prize laureate in 2003 stated in the opening of the Parliament of the World's Religions, "human rights cannot be protected with bombs" and denounced the despotic behaviour of those "who ignore human rights and democracy with the argument of belonging to a different culture and shadow dictatorial regimes with religious and nationalistic arguments."

In her address speech Ebadi defended that Islam is compatible with respect for human rights and democracy and showed her disagreement with the Islamic declaration of Human Rights. In her opinion, "if each of the 5,000 religions of the world made their own declaration this would be the end of the Universal Declaration of Human Rights."

She went on to state, "God has made human beings different but the ultimate goal of all religions is the pursuit of happiness and thus all religions can share the things they have in common."

We attended as many dialogue sessions as we could, sometimes together and other times separately. But we always met for lunch at the same place—The Parliament by the Sea. This was a tent city set up on the seashore of the sea by the Sikh community of Birmingham, U.K. Here volunteers from the Sikh community ages 16 to 60 first welcomed people, then poured water on their hands, gave people headscarves and served lunch, drinks and water to almost 6000 people a day. They also invited participants to pray in their scared spaces tent. My longing for 'desi' food was quenched with pooris, daal, chawal and achaar.

Our presentation was slotted for Saturday July 10 at 11:30 and we arrived there early—nervous because we had no way of knowing how many people would attend. To our delight a trustee from PWR came to introduce our session and told us how important it was to acknowledge the work we are doing—wow we felt honoured. Our room filled up soon with diverse people including some Barcelona Muslims. Karen, Barb and I spoke about the work we do and why we do it. At the end of our session, we distributed little boxes with a Canadian maple syrup candy, a Canada pin and a message saying "Pray for Peace—Act for Peace" while we played a song called "People of the Boxes" from the CD "The Prophet's Hands". Later people came up to ask us questions. A man wearing an Arab dress and a kufi, came to me, blessed me for the work we do and to my surprise, had tears running down his face as he said, "you make me proud to be Muslim". It wasn't the only time in Barcelona that I felt touched to tears.

The same evening, the City of Barcelona has arranged for "A Communities Night" so that people of faith could meet their own communities in different parts of the city. Barbara and I went to Ramlas Raval and met the Barcelona Muslim community. There is a large Arab and Pakistani community active in Barcelona and the

Imams of two mosques gave talks condemning violence and terrorism which was heartening to hear and even more heartening to hear that after the Madrid train bombing, people of all faiths had joined together in Barcelona and done candlelight vigils for peace. We then went and feasted on Pakistani food at the Taj Mahal Restaurant and had real 'chai' for the first time since our visit.

Next night, there was a Sacred Music concert at the Sagrada Familia (The Sacred Family) Cathedral, which is one of the most outstanding landmarks of Barcelona built by renowned architect Antoni Gaudi and still unfinished. It's an awe-inspiring structure and this was the venue to the concert where ten religious traditions presented music, movement, meditation and chants. It was an unforgettable experience sitting under the clear skies, while the Cathedral resonated with the sounds of the Cor Gospel of Barcelona; Ang singing from India; Sheva, a Jewish-Muslim band with roots in Hebrew, Arabic and Tribal cultures and Ushaq—the rich musical legacy of the Sufi Mevlevi order. As the Sufis started chanting Allah Hu, there was a hush, and then a few people joined in and I trembled as I heard the more than half the audience chanting with the Sufis. The concert ended with 10 children of 10 traditions holding up peace lights.

And of course there is Barcelona—the City of stunning and unusual architecture. We spent a day touring the city on a typical on/off bus tour so we could wander. From the Place de Catalunya, we visited The Old Quarter, Guell Park, Montjuic, Palau Reial and went crazy shopping at the Poble Espanyol which is a Spanish village built in 1929 with full scale replicas of traditional Spanish architecture. Here I was able to stroll the streets and squares of Al-Andalus and Cordoba.

As the Parliament of the World's Religions came to a close after a week of debates centered around commitments on the issues of religious violence, access to safe water, the fate of refugees worldwide, and the elimination of developing countries' debts, religious leaders who convened the gathering deemed the event a success.

The Council for a Parliament of the World's Religion's Executive Director Dirk Ficca said that one fundamental difference between this gathering and others discussing the same subjects was that, "when people of faith commit to address religious violence and other pressing issues facing the global community they follow through. We make a commitment not only to the world, but out of a deeply rooted religious or spiritual conviction. That is what makes the Barcelona Parliament commitments so special, and why this year's Parliament in Barcelona is going to make an impact."

Stepping Stones on My Journey

I am at Vancouver School of Theology where I am privileged to be part of a group that is the first visiting faculty for their interfaith summer school. The location by is by the sea and I can see the sun setting over the water while there is a lone tree where eagles have made their nest and they come and perch on the tree. The locale is totally conducive to a spiritual realm of nature, the people here being no less spiritual. I feel at home. Dr. Wendy Fletcher who is VST Principal and Dean writes in her welcome: "Some years ago I was privileged to spend a brief time in contemplation in an ancient Buddhist monastery in Southern China. One elder monk who had journeyed in that place for many years was asked by we who waited "How does one find one's path?" After a long silence he replied: "Our lives lay stretched out before us like a series of random stepping stones. We may choose only those stones we can reach with the stretch of our limbs. We reach out and test and touch and eventually make a decision. We step. If the stone holds us—life. If the stone cannot hold us and we find ourselves sinking with water rising upto our necks, we need not fear. Reaching with our arms we grasp the next stone and carry on. There is nothing to fear. In risking we see that everywhere is home".

Being Part of a Sacred Ritual

At Iona Pacific tonight I attended a celebration of 25 years of the VST Native Ministries Program. This is celebrated with a salmon BBQ and gospel jamboree. Elders and children from various indigenous groups who have been staying here to learn and teach were invited along with visiting faculty. Outside under a white tent on a beautiful crisp evening we sat around the labyrinth in the middle of which stood a lone large drum. The Rev. Dr. Martin Brokenleg who is from the Lakota clan and is a warrior, healer, educator and Vice President and Co-Founder of Reclaiming Youth International and

Director of the VST Native Ministries Program welcomed us. The amazing and unique quality of this event was the stress on culture, an expression of thanks for each part of the evening and the stories of their traditions.

We were told the story of the drum. In the Lakota tradition Dr. Martin told us there is no concept of time—only rhythm—everything has a rhythm. So drumming is a very important component of the culture. This drum was dedicated to his brother and named Oyataywanjiho—one people. We heard the story that many years ago the Sioux and Lakota were enemies and fought constantly until there was a need for peace and a way to find alliance. One native elder saw a vision in which he was asked to undertake an 8-day fast. He took some young warriors with him on a fast and while he was fasting he saw a vision of a woman who said he needs to fashion a drum upon exact specifications. The two young warriors helped make that drum and this drum signified a gift from the spirit world but a sacrifice had to be made in return (for everything they are given, they must give back in return something) so the two young men passed on to the spirit world once they completed the drum. The Sioux, Cree and Soto clans got together to give the drum a voice and made peace together by each holding one end of the drum with one hand while drumming with the other. It is said that the sound of the drum moves the spirit to peace and they made peace.

As we participated in sacred native ceremonies, the drum was central to all the rituals. Even a small tradition like making offerings was done to a drum beat and those who donated danced to the beat of the drum. Later I was given one of the greatest honours and respect in the community by being invited to count the offerings.

Young kids from the various clans came with their mothers and most often, grandmothers so arrangements were made for them to be there so the grandmothers could learn along with the kids. Everyone was given a gift and everyone joined in the circle of life. When they sang native songs, they said these were not for them—they were to give away. And they truly gave away to us their spirit of oneness with nature and of their closeness to the creator through their reverence for creation.

It is an experience I will always cherish and I am blessed and grateful that I could be here to participate in such a profound ceremony.

Rumifest Rocked

> *All this singing—just one song.*
>
> *Rumi*

A Rumi Fest took place at the Trinity-St. Paul Center in the heart of Toronto. As a start the venue spoke to the spirituality of Rumi because it's a heritage building called a Centre for Faith, Justice and the Arts. More than 750 eager Rumi fans and some just plain curious, from across North America came to this historical Church to experience Rumi. From the word go, it was a heartfelt Rumi experience. Guests were welcomed with pieces of Turkish delights, plaques of Sufi poetry, Rumi-inspired art exhibits by The Open Easel, Books and CD's on Sufism displayed by The Canadian Sufi Cultural Center, and strains of soulful Sufi music.

The main attraction of this event was Dr. Coleman Barks who flew in from Athens, Georgia. Dr. Barks has the distinct credit of introducing Mevlana Jelaluddin Rumi, the 13th Century Saint, teacher, mystic and poet to North American audiences. He has translated 15 books of Rumi and has dedicated the past two years for his magnum opus—The Big Red Book—a translation of Rumi's Mathnavi which was available for sale and signing. Dr. Barks has been reciting Rumi for over twenty years but his deeply resonant voice only improves with time. For those who heard him then and now, it's clear that he has aged to perfection and evolved into a Sufi. Dr. Barks' lifework express ecstasy with an openness, whimsy, and practicality that make the everyday resonate with the sacred; that make the everyday holy. The audience couldn't get enough of him. Against a classical background of pipes, organs and stained glass windows, Dr. Barks told stories, read poetry, chanted, laughed and recited. He was accompanied on the Cello by Anne Bourne who is a talent unto herself. Without much rehearsal, the two of them connected as though they were soul mates. Ms. Bourne would pick up where he left off and vice versa until her lilting voice, and the deep bass voice of Dr. Barks soared to the highest rafters of this stunning church sanctuary creating an ambiance that was breathtaking.

There were other artists who also added to this spiritual event bringing the best of their talent and spirit. Garo Altinian presented Rumi through Turkish and English songs, accompanied by profound poetry. He was accompanied by Agah Ecevit on the ney; Fatih Tandogan on the Bander (frame drum); Amir Amiri on the Santur, Rafi Karsli on frame drum and Leslie Gabriel Mezei reciting vocals.

Following this the audience was mesmerized and regaled with an extraordinary rendition of Rumi by Irshad Khan, who is one of the best musicians of today. He has been called the Mozart of India, and his contribution to this event was to sing Rumi in English on Sitar accompanied on Duff (frame drum)—a first. Irshad Khan got a standing ovation and the audience didn't want him to leave. But there was more.

The Jerrahi Sufi Order of Canada were the grand finale of this amazing night. They took the stage with their musical instruments ranging from Ney to bander, santur, cello, violin and vocals, they performed zikr to the most uplifting and spiritual musical accompaniment while their Shaikh Tevfik Adoner chanted verses and poetry. Two of their sema-zens had driven in from USA and they whirled for almost one hour. The audience was mesmerized and one person was heard to say that there had to be some higher presence for them to be able to whirl the way they did. The Jerrahi Sufis got a standing ovation for more than 5 minutes as the program ended on a high note through eloquent closing remarks presented by Dr. Fuad Sahin who is recipient of the Order of Ontario and an age-old practitioner of the spiritual path of Islam.

The Masks of God

By Patrick Louch, July 23, 2007

Throughout the time of Humankind,
peoples of every race,
Believed in gods of every kind,
Each with a different face.

At the core of each belief is myth,
and they point to salvation.
But if you look a little closer,
you'll see the diversity of creation,

So, it is easy to comprehend
why God has many faces.
Just look around at all the people
who make up our global races.

Each face a mask.
Each mask a voice.
And the song they sing is One.

It started in the beginning
and continues to this day,
This song is meant for everyone,
to no matter whom you pray.

Yahweh, Krishna, Buddha too,
Their voices sing the same old tune.
Be mindful of your actions,
Have courage as you walk.

Be mindful of the Golden Rule,
before you talk your talk.
For what you do, comes back to you
We are of the same Image.

Each one of us, Each God above,
and below we are all in it.
Each Plant, Each Stone, our Rock n'Roll,
We are the Light that's Living.

Brahman, Vishnu, Jesus Christ,
and Islams' Allah too,
Have shared the secrets,
to live a life,
They've told us what to do.

Move forward without Expectation,
and do not fear your life.
Seek Knowledge, Wisdom, Compassion, Truth,
move forward with this in mind.

Do whatever, is to be done,
Hold out a balanced hand.
We are all one with Spirit,
and Spirit is one with Man.
For Yin & Yang, & White & Black,
and everything in between,

Is all a part of what we See,
as well as that Un-seen.
For all we are, All that is,
Is a dream within a dream.

And the dreamer, God, like you and me,
wears many masks
Throughout our days in space and time,
answering the questions that we ask.

Move forward without Expectation,
and do not fear the Light.
Seek Knowledge, Wisdom, Compassion, Truth,
move forward with this Sight.

Do whatever is to be done,
hold out a balanced hand.
We are all one with Spirit,
and Spirit is one with Man.

Epiphany Explorations

Few years ago I was a guest speaker at Epiphany Explorations hosted by The First Metropolitan United Church in Victoria BC. Since then they have become sort of extended family and invited me again this year to Epiphany Explorations 2011—spiritual nurturing and continuing education for your personal journey. Their motto is Listen, Learn, Laugh, Sing and my journey to the center of my soul, fit right in there between spiritual nurturing and learn. So here I am seeing crosses in the sky again as signs of something profound and mysterious in my life journey.

Fact that my 61st. Birthday fell on January 21 was not lost on my hosts. I was the keynote speaker on Friday, the day of my birthday and my topic was gender in Islam. I couldn't think of a more appropriate mention on the day of my birth. Before I took the podium to speak, there was music on stage and then 500 people sang Happy Birthday for me with words that were more than the lyrics of just a song—they sang for God to protect me and keep me safe and honoured me with presents. It was a profound moment with my new found family of caring, loving and faithful people. Megumi Matsuo Saunders, wife of the Minister Allan Saunders said a profound and meaningful prayer for me, naming me directly in an invocation to God which moved me to tears.

The entire conference is well organized and well attended with notable speakers like Stephen Lewis two years ago and this year Nontombi Naomi Tutu, daughter of Desmond Tutu, Lois Wilson , Mardi Tinadal and others giving their best. After my talk a young Somali girl who is from a refugee camp and being cared for by a Church attendee, asked me if leadership for women is forbidden in the Quran. I called her up on stage and said she had all the markings of a leader and no, its not forbidden in the Quran. As a matter of fact, Belqees (Queen of Sheba) is mentioned as a leader among women. The young lady said she wants to study so she can become

Prime Minister of her country one day to bring about change. What a vision for one so young and what an inspiration for all of us. The audience gave her a standing ovation and support and she left with a wide smile and a new confidence in her step.

In my workshop I showed the film Sufi Soul narrated by William Darylmple and directed by Simon Broughton. For hundreds of millions of Sufi followers worldwide, music is at the heart of their tradition and a way of getting closer to God. From the Whirling Dervishes of Turkey to the qawwali music of Pakistan, Sufism has produced some of the worlds most spectacular music celebrated by Muslims and non-Muslims alike. Dalrymples film traces the shared roots of Christianity and Islam in the Middle East and discovers Sufism to be a peaceful, tolerant and pluralistic bastion against fundamentalism. The participants in my workshop were mesmerised and surpirsed that they had not heard of this before. There were many questions and it was very well received.

The beauty of being here again after two years was when one of the Ministers came to me and said that his congregation decided to do something last Ramadan. They read the Quran with the help of a young Muslim girl who read it in Arabic and they read it in English and he said to me "we should have done this a long time ago—how much we learnt". He then told me that one of the young men had accepted Islam and told them that they must read the Quran. He looked at me and said, "I wanted to let you know that it's because of your talk on Islam".

Its times like this that I give a word of thanks to Allah for taking me on this path where one drop in the ocean keeps me going for the next year.

Victoria is one of the most beautiful and peaceful cities in Canada and the people are warm and friendly. I will return.

Have Yourself a Merry Muslim Christmas

December is a poignant month for us as this is when my family landed in Canada 22 years ago. Christmas lights and the ambience of the season made our adjustment very cheerful, despite the challenges of the freezing weather and being new settlers.

However this is not the only reason we hold the Christmas season near and dear to us. Our association with this celebration goes far back into our childhood, when political correctness wasn't a word we were familiar with.

My husband studied in a boarding school in Pakistan and spent his winter holidays at the home of his best friend Ahmed. Ahmed's mother was Christian and celebrated her faith with gusto. On Dec 24 she would ask the boys to accompany her to church for midnight mass and Sohail remembers the beauty of the readings, the lilting music of the choir and of course the treats. Next day there would be visits and exchange of gifts and sometimes a tree because Christmas trees were hard to find in the boons of Rawalpindi. All this happened as naturally as celebrating Muslim festivals of Eid in the same house.

Similarly, I grew up in Pakistan studying in convent schools which were administered by Catholic nuns mostly from Ireland and UK. Some of my best friends were Catholics from Goa. Christmas was an exciting time because there were new and different traditions to learn from, different food to taste and gifts to give. At the time we were growing up in Pakistan (the 1960's and early 70's) there was no restriction on Christmas celebrations and churches thrived. Being a curious young person I insisted on going to church with my friends and found the experience of prayer very heart warming. It helped that we had learned the Lord's Prayer in school and know it by heart. I still remember helping my Christian friends make a nativity display and the persona of Mary has always fascinated me, doubly confirmed when I read the chapter on Mary in the Qur'an.

We knew then as we do now, that Jesus is revered as a Prophet in the Qur'an and mentioned by name more times than our own Prophet Mohammad. What we have learnt since then is that Jesus sets an example that we all need to learn from. We are told stories in the Qur'an of the virgin birth and of the miracles Jesus performed. So if Christmas is celebrated as the birth of this great messenger of God, then it's incumbent on us to commemorate it as well.

Both my husband and I feel we should utilize these days to study the life of Jesus in more detail as he was a role model for humanity. His humility, compassion and healing are great lessons for us in this time of warfare and violence.

In our early years in Canada when my sons were small in school, Christmas was still a celebration and I clearly recall going to their school to join in carol singing. However, it saddens me to see how the sanctity of Christmas has either become too commercialised, or sidelined from the faith perspective due to political correctness and not being able to fully call Christmas what it is.

Today Canada is home to a multitude of faiths making this the most diverse mosaic in the world. But we must be mindful not put the celebrations of the host community on the back burner so that we can celebrate our own. I find it disturbing that some schools and institutions have taken the "merry" out of Christmas.

So I would like to take this opportunity to wish Canadians a very Merry Christmas.

The Spirit of Ramzan

Growing up in Pakistan, my grandmother lived with us. When she became old and frail she couldn't fast in the month of Ramzan, so she used to weep. (Ramzan is the ninth month of Islamic lunar calendar in which able-bodied Muslims must refrain from food and drink from dawn till dusk everyday for a month—In Toronto, Ramzan started on Monday October 27).

As a young child to whom feasting meant more than fasting, I couldn't understand why *Daadiama* (endearment for grandmother) was unhappy when she could eat all she wants. She would say, "I don't know if I'll live to receive the blessing of another Ramzan and I want to make the most of these special days." So she would wake us for the pre-dawn meal, insisting we read the Koran. (The Koran was revealed to Prophet Mohammad in the month of Ramzan) *Daadiama* told us that the message of the Koran is to be a source of awakening and enlightenment. She would recite special invocations and prayers all day long. Her favorite prayer was: "O Allah bestow on me in this month wisdom to have mercy on orphans and to feed the hungry and keep the company of the righteous. I appeal to thee in the name of Thy benevolence. O, the shelter of the destitute, the Beneficent and Merciful."

Since *Daadiama* was elderly and on medication, she was exempt from fasting (as are travelers, pregnant or breastfeeding women, the infirm and young children). However it was incumbent on her to make arrangements for a poor person to be fed throughout the month of Ramzan. *Daadiama* insisted that she would personally prepare the early morning and evening meal for this less fortunate person and arranged for someone to come to the house and join us for the two meals everyday. This person and anyone else passing by, were our guests for meals, because *Daadiama* would say "in Ramzan the doors to hell are closed, the devil is on vacation and doors to heaven are wide open, so vie with each other to do good."

As I grew older and started fasting regularly, I understood that this practice, which is one of the five pillars of Islam, is not about giving up food, rather about self control, good thoughts & actions, charity, retrospection and reflection—a sort of annual 'servicing-of-the-soul'. I realized that I'm not allowed to be crabby because I haven't had my morning caffeine, nor lie, cheat or say a harsh word—so a smile and happy face was part of the deal. (In Ramzan fasting Muslims are supposed to eat before sunrise and after sunset everyday for 29 or 30 and then celebrate their largest festival called Eid.)

During those days of fasting long ago, the best part was the preparation and intention of making this a special time of sharing and caring. We would wake up before dawn and see twinkling lights come on in homes all around. It was such a warm feeling of solidarity. Even in those early morning hours, when stars still shone and the sky was dark, people would exchange pleasantries and food. The smell of 'parathas' (fried bread) would waft in the air. Special radio programs resounded with the sound of Koran recitation and we waited until the sound of the Azaan (call to prayer) to make our intention for fasting each day and to stop eating. Some of us went back to sleep—others used the early morning peace and quiet to pray and reflect.

Life would get back to normal during the day—kids went to study, while elders went to work. It was strange how the entire ambience and atmosphere changed—there was a feeling of spirituality in the air. I understand why fasting is called the 'invisible worship' because there's no one to check and see if we eat or drink something. One could easily hide in a corner and eat—but despite our hunger and thirst, none of us did. It was the unwritten understanding and covenant with God that kept us going. Support from people around us was a great boon because everyone was involved in the same practice.

I'm especially nostalgic for the hustle bustle before the opening of the fast at sunset. Usually it was a longish day because we didn't have the benefit of daylight savings time. An hour or so before sunset, the flurry of activity increased as *Dadiamma* perched on a chair giving loud instructions. Someone was sent off to buy *'jaleebis'* (a special sweet fried and dipped in syrup) and told strictly to ensure they were fresh and crisp, another person would be delegated to prepare milk with ground almonds and a third person could be in charge of dates (usually used to open the fast for instant energy). The air would be filled with the tempting odors of *samosas* and *pakoras* (East Indian snacks). Everything had to be co-coordinated for a specific time—the call to prayer and the siren that went off indicating it was time for opening of the fast. Even then, it was amazing to note that no one attacked the food with vengeance although you felt like eating the whole table. This was a time when one had a chance to reflect on those less fortunate, the poor and hungry, those facing wars and famine. We said a prayer and then we ate. After food there were more congregational prayers so the path to spirituality was well chalked out, taking away the focus from food to faith.

Before coming to Canada I spent a few years in Dubai, near the Arabian Sea. Here Ramzan was a joy and totally different from Pakistan. People worked only from 8a.m. to 1 p.m., at which time everyone slept and the city closed down. At sunset, everything and everyone came to life and the city shone like a star, with stores and malls open all night. Tents with sparkling chandeliers were set up along the beach, where people would come for tea and treats. Masjids (place of worship) stayed open all night for those who wished to spend their night praying—fasting was a religious, social, political and commercial event in the true sense.

As I recall those Ramzans of the past, I miss *Daadiama*. Today I can fully understand her angst. I'm diabetic and exempt from fasting but acceptance hasn't been easy. I feel left out and isolated so I'm trying to follow in *Daadiama's* footsteps by participating on the spiritual level. I still work staggered hours and wake up before dawn. My family tells me I don't have to, but this is my contribution to Ramzan. I've increased my work in the interfaith community and hope to spend valuable time with my family, reflecting on the meaning of the Koran and pondering its message to find enlightenment and enrichment.

For Muslims in Canada, perhaps this Ramzan is much more reflective of where they are at, as they continue to face challenges and their faith is put to test. This is a time when their loyalty is being questioned, and their civil rights suppressed. Some young Muslims are incarcerated; others are facing trials and our hearts go out to them. Perhaps this is also a time when Muslims realize that Ramzan prepares them to face trials and tribulations with patience, self control and forbearance—the very spirit of Ramzan.

Diversity, Transformation and Hope

> *What a joy, to travel the way of the heart.*
> *Mevlana Rumi*

A month ago I was invited by the Centre for Christian Studies to their 130th Anniversary celebrations in Winnipeg. The theme of the evening was Diversity, Transformation and Hope. I was to substitute for a great speaker Joy Kogawa, poet and author who could not make it, and I was terrified that I would never be able to fill her shoes. But when I heard the title, it was like a calling. This is me, I thought and said yes immediately.

I was thrilled to find out that I would be in dialogue with a Native elder, Stan McKay originally from Fisher River First Nation Reserve in northern Manitoba. As a child he attended Fisher River Indian Day School and the Birtle Indian Residential School. Stan's adult life has been focused on teaching and spiritual guidance as a source of healing for individuals and for communities. He is known widely as a wise teacher and elder, striving to educate Canadians about the consequences of colonialism in Canada, and especially the policy of assimilation and residential schools, and to bring about healing to the deep harm caused to Indigenous and non-Indigenous Canadians alike.

I left on this journey asking as always for signs. I took this opportunity to carry my books on Rumi as I do most of my reading on long flights. It was a beautiful, bright autumn day with a blue sky and cumulous clouds and I saw many formations of crosses as I have been wont to do for many years. (I've finally concluded that its' God sending me kisses!) I arrived at my hotel in Winnipeg and was dumbstruck to see the telephone number being the numerical code for Bismillah—I begin in the name of God. (Front Desk: 1-204-786-

7011) Furthermore the stationary in the hotel room had the words hope embossed on them. I had my signs and any trepidation I had about entering a new place, new people, doing my first ever speaking stint without written notes, was allayed. I felt rejuvenated, inspired, anxious, and hopeful all at once.

Rightly so. When I reached the venue of the event, I was amazed at how many people I knew from my 15 years of interfaith work across Canada. We met and hugged like old friends. Stan and I met privately in a room to connect. And connect we did. As tradition deems, I had taken Stan a gift of tobacco and I gave it to him privately but he decided to inform the audience as he was so thrilled. The audience was primarily women, mostly Christian but with a smattering of Native youth, and later I discovered some Muslims.

I had decided to take Rumi as my muse and Stan brought a book of reading titled 'God is Red" which he is mailing me as a gift. I also took a CD of Sufi chanting which was played as people came into the hall. We were supposed to be in a facilitated dialogue but as we sat facing each other and started talking, the 250+ audience faded away and it seemed we were two souls speaking as one. Facilitator and friend Betsy Anderson from Emmanuel College found herself with nothing to do—Stan and I clicked heart-to-heart and shared ruminations, readings and Rumi.

I read a universal blessing from Rumi and Stan shared a story about dreams. I have been fascinated since my arrival in Canada with the Native ethos, which to me corresponds deeply with the spiritual message of my faith, drowned in the din of dogma. Stan shared that the native communities are very diverse and there is sometimes very little intra-faith dialogue although inter-faith dialogue thrives and I was able to tell him the same for our communities. He asked me about diversity within the Islamic faith and he and the audience were surprised when I explained the different denominations and sects in Islam as they did not know. We agreed that unity does not mean uniformity and that diversity is a divine blessing. However we also agreed that people can't be forced to 'like' each other and move into a group hug as long as differences are recognized and respected.

I shared the following reading on diversity from Rumi:

*Every war and every conflict between human beings
has happened because of some disagreement about
names.*

*It is such an unnecessary foolishness,
because just beyond the arguing
there is a long table of companionship
set and waiting for us to sit down.*

*What is praised is one, so the praise is one too,
many jugs being poured into a huge basin.
All religions, all this singing, one song.
The differences are just illusion and vanity.*

*Sunlight looks a little different on this wall
than it does on that wall
and a lot different on this other one,
but it is still one light.*

*We have borrowed these clothes,
these time-and-space personalities,
from a light, and when we praise,
we are pouring them back in.*

Stan and I then shared our thoughts on transformation. Stan spoke of the painful experiences of Colonization and the residential schools. He shared that the wounds have been deep leaving much conflict in the Native communities, especially among the youth who are angry and need to find ways to channel their anger, a concept that resonated with me. He spoke about his own transition from anger to hope and peace. The key here is recognizing that a wrong has been done in history, creating awareness of it and then working towards forgiveness. The official movement for this is the Truth and Reconciliation Commission which I have been part of and not a co-incidence, their pin is also a circle.

Stan told a wonderful story about a grandfather who tells his grandson that each one of us have two wolves in our being. One is good, the other is evil. Grandson asks, which wolf is the stronger and wise grandfather replies "the one you feed". Wow—I loved the story as I am trying to share stories with my own grandsons, a tradition we have forgotten but over time I've collected many stories so they listen in fascination. It was a reminder to me that we need to bring back a story-telling tradition, one found among the Sufis.

I shared that my life has been a journey of change and transformation. I am not the person I was 25 years ago and much of my journey towards spirituality has been in Canada as I find myself free to pursue the different paths that lead to the same Creator. Change is positive, we agreed and since the world is changing so fast in so many ways, if we want to be part of the larger change, we need to transform ourselves as well. The journey for both of us is an ongoing saga in our lives, bringing hope, hostility and happiness. But as Rumi says:

If you could, what could you do?
This being human is a guest-house.

Every morning a new arrival.
A joy, a depression, a meanness,
some momentary awareness
comes as an unexpected visitor.

Welcome and entertain them all!
Even if they're a crowd of sorrows,

Who violently sweep your house,
empty of its furniture.

Still, treat each guest honorably.
He may be clearing you out for some new delight.

The dark thought, the shame, the malice,
meet them at the door laughing, and invite them in.

Be grateful for whoever comes,
because each has been sent as a guide from beyond.

On growth Rumi says "If you are irritated by every rub, how will your mirror be polished?" How can we learn, live and grow to become our greatest aspirations if every opportunity for growth is an irritant? Not that it is easy to be on the receiving end all that polishing. But the result, ahh the results, they are the reason we pursue situations where we can be polished"

We spoke of hope and I shared that I'm an eternal optimist and for me the glass is always half full. Stan works in healing circles and shared his hopes. The concept of circle is universal. The logo of the CCS is a circle, the Aboriginal people are very circle oriented and the Sufis embrace circle as the circle of life. Our connections were getting stronger by the moment. Stan asked me to share stories from the Islamic faith about the environment and I felt so blessed to be able to share the spiritual message of my faith, which most in the audience had never heard, thanks to hysteria and news about the extremists taking over the news. Stan felt exactly the same has happened in his life and we were honoured to be able to showcase the spiritual messages.

By Allah, we must always have hope. Faith, itself, consists of fear and hope. Someone once asked me, "Hope itself is good, but what is this fear?" I said, "Show me a fear without hope, or a hope without fear. The two are inseparable." For example, a farmer plants wheat. Naturally he hopes that wheat will grow. At the same time he is afraid some blight or drought may destroy it. So, there is no hope without fear, or fear without hope.

After an hour of interaction, we stopped for Q & A, although we felt we could have talked all night long. Later there was a reception at which a young Iranian girl came up and said how inspired she felt.

When there's no sign of hope in the desert,

So much hope still lives inside despair.

Heart, don't kill that hope:

Even willows bear

Sweet fruit in the garden of the soul.

All This Singing, Just One Song

On a beautifully clear, full moon night a few Sundays ago, an incredible event took place at the Harbour front Theatre in Toronto.

An Israeli born musician alternately played the acoustic guitar and a Bansuri (flute) accompanied by two gypsy folksingers who played the Harmonium, Table and traditional Rajasthani instruments called Khirtal, Bhapand & Morchang. This was Shye Ben Tzur with Kutle Khan and Chugge Khan straight from the deserts of Rajasthan singing Quawwali (a form of Sufi devotional from South Asia) in Hebrew and Urdu as they performed for the Ashkenaz Festival in Toronto—their first performance in North America.

How did this come about? I was so fascinated by the fusion and passion of this eclectic group that I took time to meet the main composer and musician Shye Ben Tzur and a fascinating story emerged.

Tzur, 35grew up in Tel Aviv composing and playing rock music and heading a band called Sword of Damocles. He was only 19 when he attended his first Indian concert as Pandit Hari Prasad Chaurasia and Ustad Zakir Hussain performed in Jerusalem and he fell in love with the sound of the flute and Tabla. Tzur says he was always fascinated by mystical poetry and had read the works of Rumi and Attar (Sufi poets) but he felt an urge to find out more about Indian music. "The music was calling me".

He left home with no idea where he would go and took a flight to Benares, India. "I didn't know anything about India but for some reason I thought this was a city full of music and I will find a teacher here". He found India but not a music teacher and feeling depressed one day he went into a bookstore looking for poetry "to uplift my heart" he says. He bought a book on mystical music by HazratInayat Khan, founder of The Sufi Order of the West (http://www.hazrat-inayat-khan.org) and it made him even more committed to his search for a teacher of mystic music. Continuing his search, Tzur came to

Delhi and was directed to the Dergah of HazratNizamuddinAulia (www.nizamuddinaulia.com) a famous Sufi Saint. Tzur says "I know Sufis loved music so I came here looking for teacher because I naively thought everyone is a musician and they would know!" From here he was guided to continue his search in Ajmer, Rajasthan.

Tzu ended up in Ajmer at the Dargah (shrine) of Hazrat Khwaja Moinuddin Chishti and had a strange encounter. He says "someone there pointed to a man and said this is the person to talk to. So I went up to the man but he would not speak and I just sat there and told him what I was searching for. We sat in silence for a few days and then he motioned me to follow him and he took me to a teacher. That was 15 years ago, and I'm still in Ajmer—learning!"

Tzur discovered that Ajmer was the place he was looking for where almost every other person was a musician who had inherited the art from his ancestors. Tzu later married a young girl from Ajmer, made it his second home and started learning about Sufi music, the language and the people. "I had always written poetry but now I was learning a new language, culture and an absolutely magical kind of music—Sufi music and I was entranced by the depth of the poetry and music." Tzur worked with a variety of poets and musicians and started translating some of the Sufi poetry into Hebrew. "My own heritage came into play and I realised that I could express myself in my native language and find beauty in it knowing that the essence is the same."

To bring his art closer to home, he taught a few Gypsy musicians Hebrew and they formed a group travelling across India performing Sufi music in Urdu and Hebrew. "We are nourished by what we know and what is around us" says Tzur as he embraces the best of both worlds—Israel and India. His family came to visit him in India and supports his work.

His first concert in Israel was called "Heeyam" and got great reviews so Tzur and his troupe of eight musicians and singers started travelling between Israel and India bridging the gap between the two countries and cultures with music. He has another album called

"Shoshan". In 2004, he performed at Jahan-e-Khusru, the prestigious international Sufi music festival held in New Delhi in the spring annually since 2001.

When Tzur is on stage wearing traditional Indian Sherwani with a Rajasthani scarf, he blazes with fire and passion; his words resonate as he translates from Hebrew to English and from Urdu to Hebrew for his audience without missing a beat. Yet in person backstage he is shy, humble and soft spoken—a true mystic at heart. He is inspired by Hazrat Khwaja Moinuddin Hasan Chishti popularly known as Khwaja Gharib Nawaz and he says "I'm a musician and Khwaja Gharib Nawaz brings me to life, teaching me about 'onenesses as the essence of life".

Today he makes his home in two countries and plans to "keep on finding new and different ways to present Sufi poetry in both languages".

The Muslim New Year: A Time for Reflection

> *Today, Muslims look upon the incident at Karbala as an example of good over evil; of justice over injustice; of truth over falsehood and of bravery over cowardice.*

While most cultures and religions ring in their new year with feasts, celebrations and parties, the Islamic new year brings with it deep contemplation and reflection. Today is the first of Moharram (the first month of the Muslim calendar) and the onset of the Islamic new year –

Hijra (Hijra meaning migration.) Dating from the time that the messenger of Islam, Prophet Mohammed (peace be upon him), migrated from his birthplace Mecca to Medina in Saudi Arabia (approximately 619 A.D.), the Muslim calendar is lunar, and consists of twelve months.

In the year 61 Hijra (680 A.D.) an incident took place in Karbala, Iraq, that shook the foundations of the religion of Islam. To this day, Karbala is cited by International Historians as the most tragic incident of sacrifice and valour in the History of the world. It was fifty years after the death of Prophet Mohammad and the religion of Islam as taught by him, was being faithfully practiced and preached by his family and disciples. However, politics had started to invade the purity and simplicity of the faith. Political power of the Caliphate shifted to the Omayyads who were mercenaries and were eager to rule over the fast growing Muslim Empire. Yazid, a tyrant known to be against truth, justice and all the good that Islam stood for, wanted to become king of all Muslims. He demanded allegiance from everyone by force, but Hussain, grandson of the Prophet resisted him. Hussain was well respected by the Muslim community and commanded a great following. He was known to be a peace loving man and Yazid thought that if he could scare or coerce Hussain into accepting him, he would become the unchallenged ruler of all Muslims.

Hussain was aware that the life of his supporters was endangered by refusing allegiance to Yazid. So he decided to go to Kufa (a small town in Iraq) with 72 followers, all of whom were against the despotism of Yazid. Yazid got wind of the trip and intercepted the group on the banks of the Euphrates, at the plains of Karbala. Once again Yazid demanded that Hussain and his followers pledge allegiance to him, but Hussain was a righteous man and he refused to bow down to pressure. He opted to stand up for justice and rebel against the hypocrisy of Yazid, even if it meant putting his small group of followers at risk.

While Hussain camped in the plains of Karbala, asking only to be allowed to pray in peace and reach Kufa, Yazid with an army of 30,000 soldiers cordoned off the water supply for Hussain's people leaving them thirsty and parched in the sweltering heat of the desert. Yazid then slowly and relentlessly proceeded to slaughter the small caravan of people including innocent children and infants.

The Battle of Karbala was a clash not between personalities, but between two principles—love of truth against lust for power and passion for justice against perversity of tyranny. The symbols of human dignity that Islam preaches i.e. peace, humanity, tolerance, patience, brotherhood, forgiveness and equality among human beings, were in danger of being obliterated. Hussain sacrificed his life and the blood of his family to keep these qualities alive and in his death they were realised.

Today, Muslims look upon the incident at Karbala as an example of good over evil; of justice over injustice; of truth over falsehood and of bravery over cowardice. Throughout the seige at Karbala, Hussain remained calm and continued to pray with his followers. He never lost his faith in God or his religion. It would have been easy for him to submit to Yazid, but Hussain would not compromise his principles—the principles that were instilled into his soul by his father, Ali and his grandfather, Mohammad the messenger of Islam.

During the first ten days of the Muslim New Year, Muslims pray for the souls of those martyred at Karbala. Their stories of valour and courage; of mothers sending their sons into the battlefield to face certain death; of infants dying of thirst; and mostly of sacrifice and an unshakable faith, are told in mosques and homes.

On the 10th day of Moharram, Muslims in many parts of the world, relive and enact the tragedy of Karbala for it was on this day that the inhuman slaughter of Hussain and his followers was completed. It is important to take the lesson that Muslims learn from Karbala and apply it to the world today. Everywhere in the world where injustice, cruelty and inhumanity is being practiced, another Karbala is taking place. Examples are given of places like Chechnya, Rwanda, Bosnia, Kashmir. To denounce all acts of violence against humanity is what the tragedy of Karbala is all about. To relive, recant and remember through discussions, lectures and prayers, is what the Muslim New year is all about.

Letter to My Best Friend

> *After our death do not search for us in tombstones of the graveyards,*
> *But search for us in the hearts of people we have inspired.*
>
> *Rumi*

Antra,

I know you expect me to write something on the first anniversary of your death. I always wrote to you first and complained that you never write. And you always said "that's because you're a writer and you love to write. So stop whining and make sure you write me a nice obituary." Do you know how difficult it is to summarize in a few lines, the turbulent, rich, stormy, warm and vibrant friendship we had that spanned over thirty years? This, my dearest friend, soul mate and sister—is for you.......

I still remember the first day we met. I was the country 'bumpkin', new to Karachi and new to St. Joseph's college. You were among the 'elite' of the college. Well known, popular and good looking. You were also spoilt and status conscious. I don't know what made you reach out to me—maybe you took pity on my unabashed naivety in the big city—whatever it was, I was more than grateful to grab the hand of friendship extended by you. And I have never let it go.

It was a bonding of the spirit that was to last a lifetime. When I think about it in retrospect, it was a strange and unusual liaison. We were as different as summer and winter. You were unashamedly curious about people—I lived in a cocoon; I came from a conservative middle class family—you wore expensive clothes, owned exotic perfumes and were a socialite; I had many limitations on my lifestyle—you were free as a bird. But I looked up to you. You sort of took me under your wing and tried to smarten me up. I still recall the day you dragged me to the beauty parlour and had my waist length (but unruly) hair chopped to shoulder length. I looked in the mirror continuously to find the old me. You also helped me get a new wardrobe. You had a lot of say in molding my personality in those days and I accepted it because you were my friend and that was the most important thing in my life.

The fact that you were from a Bengali Hindu family and I am Muslim, did not faze us in any way. We were a strange blend—you would keep rozas and celebrate Eid with me and on your meatless days, I would share daal, bhaat with you and your family. Religion was never a bar to our friendship. Ammie accepted you as my close friend but made it clear that apart from your house, there were not too many places I could go without a chaperon. You of course, had a chaperon. Your fiancé, who you told me was a cousin!! I was so stupid, I believed you! Everyone in college except me knew what was going on. I could never understand what you saw in him but made a great effort to like him because of you. The feeling was mutual because I don't think he cared much for me either and tolerated me because of you.

Your father, Baba, on the other hand, was very fond of me. Maybe I was seeking a 'father' figure in him, because my own father was dead, the same way you subconsciously found a mother's love in Ammie. And of course, on the outlying borders of our friendship was your young brother, a pest in those days and Bebe and Bhaya (my older sister and brother) on my side. Soon you knew everyone in my family and vice-versa.

I never got a chance to tell you this, but I was committed to this friendship from the beginning. If Bhaya or Bebe tried to comment on your modern way of life, or your daring dressing, I stood up for you and supported you with all my heart and soul. I guess I had accepted that in every relationship, there has to be a 'giver' and a 'taker'. I had willingly opted to become the giver and I think, over a span of thirty odd years it remained the same. I have to admit there has been great joy in this friendship—the hours we spent talking and philosophizing about life, love and laughter. I learnt a lot about real life from you. Remember the days we would come home from college, collapse on the sofa in your house, listen to soul music and talk non-stop? Baba commented that we talk at the same time and no one listens to the other—but he was wrong. We did listen. It was very important to listen to each other because our opinions were what mattered most to us in those days. We were selfish and self-opinionated like all other teenagers.

Over a period of time, we became inseparable. We went to college, came home, shopped, gossiped, talked, studied and were together 24 hours a day. Although you had other friends, I was the permanent side to the triangle. You went to many parties where I was not allowed to go, but I was happy to just see your new clothes and hear about it from you. You had all the freedom and things that I could not have—except for a mother. You never expressed any feelings about lack of a mother in your life. I don't think you even recalled what it was like to have one because your mother had died when you were a child. However, you took to my mother and soon you were like another child in my house. In retrospect, I can see that my other two siblings were rather jealous of you and the attention you got from my mother and I. They could see that I was totally influenced by you but they did not dislike you.

You were the first one in our class to travel to England to meet your future in-laws and then get married. By this time I had accepted that your 'cousin' was really your fiancé, the dashing Dr. Anwar Ali. Your wedding was fun but traumatic. Since you had no relatives, we took it upon ourselves to get everything done. Remember how the dupatta in your shaadi ka jora didn't match the gharara? We were so scared, we didn't tell anyone! Then Ammie decided that you had to become Muslim and arrived with the Maulana on the day of your 'Mehendi'. Baba did not object because you were marrying a Muslim so your given Muslim name became Aneeta. The funniest incident was when someone called Anwar on your honeymoon and asked "Is Raheel with the two of you?"—he was livid and always related that incident, even 20 years later. Then you left for England and I was left in a vacuum without a friend to turn to. Due to the depth of our friendship, I never made another close friend. The day you left I cried and howled so much that your father and my mother were astonished at the intensity of my despair.

You settled in England and proceeded to become a "pukka" housewife. I, too got married and visited you. Luckily Anwar and Sohail hit off right away and our friendship was clinched. I found myself spending more time with you in Birmingham, than with my own siblings in Karachi. I was there for the birth of all four of your children. You used to wait for me to arrive, hand me the latest baby and say "okay, now I can sleep and Raheel khala will look after you". I loved it. I was truly a "khala" to your kids and even Anwar had grudgingly accepted me as the "saali" he never had. He always welcomed me warmly but warned me that if, in our gup shup, he missed a regular meal, there would be hell to pay. Of course, we talked nonstop and I remember that I always lost my voice in two days and Anwar would give me throat medicine and threaten us with dire consequences—but secretly he loved the hangama. Life at your house was always one big party. All your friends knew us as sisters. Every time there was a crisis in your life, you'd call me to come and do a 'Quran Khatam' and for all happy occasions, I organized the milaad for you. You were so proud of me and would immediately call everyone and announce

"Raheel is here."

You saved up all your secrets, gossip and worries to tell me and we used to talk all night. The kids were surprised at our closeness. Once your daughter, Narmeen asked us if we ever fought and I remember your telling her "the true test of our friendship is that we can say whatever we like to each other, fight and still remain best friends. You kids will never have a relationship like ours." During this period Ammie died and you grieved for her the way I did—like losing a mother, because every time she wrote to me, she used to write to you as well.

You and Anwar used to fret over my lack of kids—when I had my first son both of you rejoiced. When I was expecting my younger son, I came to you and stayed for six months. This was when Baba died in Bangladesh under stressful circumstances. You left for Dacca and met up with your brother after many years. In Baba's death, the two of you found each other again, because he was the only blood relative you had. This is when I realized how inwardly strong you are because you weathered this crisis stoically although I knew you were hurting inside.

Many good things in our life originated from your house. The birth of Zain, my younger son and our immigration to Canada are two of them. You and Anwar shared in our joy. Some of the happiest times in my life were spent with you. Across the Atlantic, our friendship grew more solid. You came to visit me, Narmeen came and of course I continued to go whenever I could.

In 1992, I saw the film "Beaches" in Toronto and I called you to see it. I recall that you immediately called me back and said that you were the one who would die and would I look after your kids? I joked "No, of course not, because if I die first, I don't want you to look after my kids". Both of us sniffled and then laughed at our own stupidity.

We had the best of times, Antra and although our relationship was not one in which we ever became sentimental with each other, I think you know how much I miss you. Not a day passes when I don't think of you or think about all the little news items I have to share with you. Your children are now the only link we have and I wish they were here with me. Maybe I didn't have daughters of my own because I your daughters like they were my own. You do know that I care for them very deeply and will always look out for them.

Perhaps the most painful thing I ever did in my life, was to put away your personal things and itemize your jewellery. I had always told your girls about the wedding dress episode and sure enough when we unpacked your shaadi ka jora after 30 years, the dupatta and gharara did not match. In your bedside drawer were letters I had written you from day one, every cutting and pictures I had sent.

That's when I knew that you also cared for me deeply as a friend and sister—but you never said anything. Among your jewellery were some pieces of your mother's that I knew you had, there were the little trinkets you had collected for your daughters and of course some jewellery that we had made alike. Your girls gave me some of your clothes which I wear with great love and reverence.

Was ours the friendship of a lifetime? I don't know. All I know is that it was unique and that you have left a vacumn in my life that no one can fill. Ours was more than a friendship—we were soul mates and soul sisters.

Farewell my friend—I miss you and I always will.

Epilogue

In May 1995, Antra was diagnosed as having low grade lymphoma with 99% chances of recovery. I went to see her and we found that we were both touchy and sensitive—we talked about the 'good ol days' and cried a lot. I sensed that this trip was different from the others but could not pin-point the problem. I came back and Antra started deteriorating but she didn't tell me. I would call and write and I worried but never even suspected that her health was so bad. She was always like a rock, strong, so alive, so overpowering—how could anything ever happen to Antra? Every time I asked Anwar, he said "she' doing well—great chance of recovery". End of October, he called and said "she's going fast. Come and see her". On October 29, Sohail and I flew to England to see her. I'll never forget the look on her face when she saw us and burst into tears. She was a skeleton—already a dead body and I was not prepared for this shock. Still her spirit was so strong that she came home from the hospital for that weekend and what a soulful and touching weekend we had with me sitting by her side the entire time. We cried a lot but she had hope. The kids were subdued and sad. When we dropped Antra at the hospital on Monday, I knew it was goodbye, but I did not say it. I hugged her for the last time, and I wanted to say "kaha suna maaf kar daina" (forgive me for what I may have said) but the words stuck in my throat.

Three weeks later, on November 23, 1995, Antra died, free from her agony and pain. I went to bid my last farewell and found myself in the agonizing process of helping prepare her 'kafan', the same way I had dressed her as a bride. Antra died a believing, practicing Muslim, and more than a thousand people attended her namaz-e-janaaza. Anwar and the children were shattered.

Nine weeks later, on February 4, 1996 Anwar died of a heart attack.
Today Anwar and Antra Ali are buried side by side in a graveyard in Birmingham where fresh flowers are put every week. They leave behind to grieve for them, Narmeen 23, Meena 19, Shehla 17, Razi 15 .... and me.

In Memoriam for My Father

Accept the things I cannot change...

My father was unique and I loved him dearly. He was a gentle, kind and sensitive man who could do no wrong in my eyes. I am the youngest of three children and although I spent the least time with him, he was a friend and a mentor.

He was a dynamic young army dentist at the time of British colonialism in the subcontinent. I have photos of him in uniform as a young army officer. He looks dashing—a bit like Errol Flynn who he admired. My grandmother said that British nurses would bat their eyelashes at this six foot plus tall, handsome young Lieutenant.

My paternal grandfather saw that Abbajaani had the makings of a playboy, so he wanted him married and settled. He chose my mother who was his favorite niece. Abbajaani did not want to get married because he relished his bachelor life. He loved to party and have a good time so he tried to avoid the match, but nothing worked against the invincible law of the family patriarchs.

They were married and posted at a small cantonment where Abbajaani immediately proceeded to woo my mother and fall in love with her. She was young, fresh and unspoilt. He taught her every nicety of growing up as the wife of a popular army Captain. Abbajaani adored my mother. I have read letters he wrote to her the first few years of their marriage in which the romantic poetry makes me blush. Ammi had my brother and sister one year apart.

I came late in my parent's life—as an unwanted addition at a bad time. From the beginning Abbajaani adored me. I loved to hear about the day I was born.

"It was a dark, stormy and cold night" he would begin dramatically. Then a smile would curl the corner of his mouth and he'd continue, "and this dark, child was born—screaming." At this point, seeing my teary face, he'd hug me and say "but she's my special princess who's brought me immense joy, and I love her more than anything in my life." I knew he meant that.

Earliest memories of my Abbajaani are warm, cosy times. Abbajaani would put me on his lap and promise, "when you grow up and become a dentist, we'll open a private practice together and you can have as many gold teeth as you want." I can still recall the warm tweedy smell of my Abbajaani's coat. He smoked a pipe with Erinmore tobacco. The mixed aroma of his aftershave and tobacco was my favorite smell.

Abbajaani taught me swimming, took me riding and wanted me to be the son he missed because he wasn't close to my brother. He would take me bicycle riding and we'd talk about everything under the sun—about life and about why no one understood him—he had his own demons to deal with. I learnt more about life and living from Abbajaani than I would have from anyone else. As a result I was mature for my age. We would go to the library and he'd insist that I read literature, philosophy, history and psychology.

On my school holidays he would take me to his dental surgery. His patients loved him, because he was gentle and caring, with precise hands and a wonderful sense of humour. He would ask me to talk to the patient's to divert their attention. I was so proud of him.

After work, he would put me on his bicycle and take me to the club where I could have mango juice and he would have a drink, which was a big no no and constantly got him into trouble although it didn't bother me.

Later my sister went to boarding school, and my brother went to America. Since I was the only one who was home, Abbajaani began to depend on me for everything to the extent that he wouldn't eat unless I was beside him. He would tell me "I want you to become famous and do something great with your life. Always reach for the stars" he advised, "and they will come down to you to fill your life with light and joy. Don't settle for mediocrity. You have the potential to achieve greatness in your life."

Another person who understood Abbajaani and stood by him unconditionally was his old army butler, Sarwar Shah who was like a family member and we could only call him Shah Sahab. Sarwar Shah had been with Abbajaani since he was a young cadet. He was a faithful valet and a friend to Abbajaani and me. When things would become really bad I used to go to Sarwar Shah and cry. He would say, "don't let Sahib see you cry because you are his strength. Go and make him laugh. Make him forget his problems and talk to you." Many nights I sat and talked with Abbajaani so he wouldn't be alone. If I ran out of words, I would recite his favorite poetry. He, in turn, had told me his life story so many times, I knew it by heart. I heard tales about his sojourn during World War 2, his times in Baghdad, his friend Joe who had a gold tooth and how he wanted to take me with him on travels to Spain so we could see the bull fights as Errol Flynn had done.

I joined college and those were the happiest days of my life. I had visions of a bright future. Every day at recess, Abbajaani would be waiting by the college gate to take me across the street to buy pastries. Ammi ranted and raved that he spoilt me. He would look at her and say gently "Hush. Please don't be harsh with her. She brings me great joy and peace."

He had a great sense of humour and fun—one day he wore a burqa and we went all over the city in a tonga laughing like kids.

It was a cold, crisp November day and I skipped to the college gate planning my gastronomical treat. News on radio was about Kennedy's assassination and the college buzzed. Instead of Abbajaani, Sarwar Shah stood there. He said we had to go home. I asked why, but he did not look at me and said those were his instructions. He took me home and fed me. After I had eaten, he said, "Sahib is gone." I thought he meant my Abbajaani had gone out. Sarwar Shah was weeping and I felt a sick kind of dread. I did not ask any questions. He took me to my uncle's house where my grandmother lived. There was a huge crowd and from the gate I could hear the women wailing.

No one paid much attention to me. Ammi and my grandmother were hysterical. I heard the words "heart attack." Through a haze I saw my brother being comforted by the men in the family, my sister sat with her arms wrapped around mother and I felt cold and alone. There was a block of ice around my chest. Sarwar Shah sensed my agony and kept holding my hand but I shrugged him away and went inside the house—searching.

My instincts guided me to a dark room, cooled with ice, in the middle of which lay a body on a single bed, covered with a white sheet. I softly padded over to the bed. Lifting the sheet I saw Abbajaani's serene face. He looked like he was asleep. I sat there and held his hand and talked to him. I patted his forehead and touched his face. It was still warm and I was convinced that there is a mistake. He was just sleeping. I don't know how long I sat there and talked to him—willing him to reply.

I heard a commotion around me and came to senses when someone tried to pry my hands away from Abbajaani. There was much distress at discovering me sitting with a dead body. Elders of the family said I was always a 'strange one' and I was reprimanded soundly for "disturbing the dead". I crept away and found Sarwar Shah blubbering like a baby in a corner of the garden. We cried unashamedly for the friend we had both lost. Abbajani has not reached his 45th birthday.

I was thirteen and a part of me died that day.

No Compulsion Here... Yet!

On a visit to Istanbul

This Thanksgiving we took a much overdue trip to Istanbul, Turkey and I feel compelled to write about what I saw. It was interesting to try and convince my grandsons that the "Turkey" we were visiting was not the same turkey they were consuming!

We had chosen a place to stay at random and it was a pleasant surprise that it turned out to be in the Old City walking distance from The Blue Mosque, Hagia Sophia and Topkapi Palace.

Having come from Canada, it was a balm to our ears to hear the Azaan (call to prayer) and we traipsed off in search of the Mosque. We had to walk through the Bazaar and it was interesting to note that not everyone rushed off to pray. Those who wished to worship, did so quietly and others stayed on the sides respectfully while those who were not in the Mosque went about their business. There was no feeling of being compelled to pray and it was a new sensation for those of us who have seen the likes of Saudi Arabia where you are beaten into submission. It also makes sense of the Quranic line "there is no compulsion in religion."

Next day we had breakfast in the hotel which by the way, served soup, salad and cheeses that kept us going all day on one meal. We met a tourist from Sweden who liked to start and end his day with local Turkish beer. Then I noticed that the corner convenience store also sold beer and raki. So it was—belly dance and beer exist side by side with Mosques and Minarets. The person who comes of the Mosque and the person who comes out of the bar meet but do not collide in the public square. Religiosity is a buzz in the background, not in your face, with no one telling you what to do or not to do— yet. You can't tell by looking at anyone where they are from as heels and hijab, short skirts and shalwars, beards and buzz cuts mix and mingle with ease.

People were happy and friendly, especially to Pakistanis which is a pleasant surprise. I kept refreshed on fresh pomegranate juice which gave energy for the whole day. Topped up with Turkish coffee, Turkish food, Turkish delight and Turkish tea—we were in culinary heaven. There are beautiful public squares with benches, everyone is kid-friendly and while it was cold for others, coming from Canada all we could say was what's cold eh?

There was a framed photo of Mustapha Kemal Ataturk in the hotel lobby and the young people who ran the hotel called themselves proud 'secular' turks. The word secular came up many times during our stay. Our young guide who took us to the Mosque of Ayub Ansari and other sites, mentioned time and again that Turkey is secular. It was also fascinating to note that none of the Mosques are lit up or heavily decorated—the old architecture from the time of the Ottomans has been kept as close to the original as possible with no ostentatious additions.

There is a strong Sufi influence even though Sufism also went underground during Ataturk's reformation towards secularism but there are enough people who follow the Tareeqas to make it a reality. I think it's due to the Sufi influence that there is a softness among Turkish Muslims which was inspiring.

However all is not what it seems on the surface. When the rallies started at Taksim square, people thought this was another incident like Tahrir Square in Egypt. Through conversations with Turks both within and outside Turkey, my understanding is that this was different. First of all Turkey is economically stable and you can see this is Istanbul so the grumblings of economically deprived masses is not the case.

Secondly they have had years of being secular and the push back, especially by young Turks was against Turkish Prime Minister Recep Tayyip Erdogan's insistence on forcing Islam into the public square. At first he made subtle moves like putting a ban on stewardesses wearing red lipstick on Turkish Airlines—the response was not so subtle. Every stewardess regardless of age wore bright red lipstick—I like that! I believe the ban was lifted.

But in September this year two dramatic announcements by Erdogan sent shivers down the spines of many of the country's secularists. Erdogan annulled a decades-long ban on wearing headscarves in public institutions and ended the daily reciting of the pledge of allegiance in primary schools.

These moves have the potential to alienate Turkey's minority non-Muslim communities. Turkish researcher Halil M. Karaveli, claimed in a New York Times op-ed that far from helping Turkey's minority, Erdogan was increasingly playing with sectarian fire. Already from 13 Synagogues, there are now only 3 left.

"Erdogan is turning Turkey into a powder keg in an attempt to shore up his own political base," Karaveli wrote. "He is intentionally activating the longstanding fault lines separating religious and secular Turks — and most dangerously the divide between the country's Sunni majority and its Alevi minority. If he continues to do so, Turkish democracy itself could become a casualty of his confrontational policies."

More recently there was a petition to turn Hagia Sophia into a Mosque and this has many Turks in a dither.

So Turkish youth come out regularly to Taksim Square to protest what they call Erdogan's dictatorship and intrusion into their private lives such as restrictions on personal freedoms; the non-availability of alcohol after 10 pm; the ban on public displays of affection and the "advice" from Erdogan for Turkish women to have "at least three children." These young Turks want "freedom" and will continue to lobby for their right to have these freedoms in a secular Turkey.

From Darkness to Light

A visit to The Canadian Museum for Human Rights (CMHR).

This past weekend I was in Winnipeg for a conference hosted by **Canadian Women for Women in Afghanistan** and on Sunday they had arranged for a visit to The Canadian Museum For Human Rights.

I had read about the controversy surrounding the opening last month, but decided that I want to see for myself what this is all about.

While at the conference, I spoke with some locals from Winnipeg and asked their opinion. Most were very supportive, but there was some hesitancy and critique—mostly from those who had not been to the Museum yet, which I found interesting. One Arab woman was quite hostile and said that the Museum did not reflect all the human rights atrocities across the globe and focused on one particular aspect. I asked if she was referring to the Holocaust exhibit and she said "yes and also the Native community is not represented". I recalled that among those who protested at the opening were the Aboriginal community and remarks were made by some Arab groups about the lack of representation for their cause. Fair enough as I had not seen the Museum yet.

However I said to the lady that if I had the vision and finances of Izzy Asper, and the opportunity to create a Human Rights Museum, I would probably have the Pakistan-India partition as one of the largest exhibits. Why? Because in my lifetime that is the event that personally impacts me. So, more power to the Asper family for making the Holocaust exhibit front and center as we all need to remember.

As we walked through CMHR, the first thing I noted was that the building itself speaks of human rights. Antoine Predock, winner of the coveted American Institute of Architects Gold Medal has built a most unusual structure. It's an awe-inspiring experience as you start at the lower level which is quite dark and walk over various ramps to the top and as you go up, you keep finding more light until you reach the top where there is a tower of hope and a panoramic view of Winnipeg (quite the change from the flat, dull view from my hotel window). The architecture throughout is not beautiful but stunning in its starkness and the play of light and darkness, making us acutely aware that human rights are fragile and need to be protected.

After our tour of the building, we were taken to a classroom where two Directors from the Museum took us through a powerpoint presentation of the exhibits that are already in place and those that are planned for November and beyond. This presentation was created with a special segment for Canadian Women for Women in Afghanistan because with their input, the Afghanistan exhibit has been enhanced. At the end of the presentation, one elderly Afghan woman stood up and tearfully thanked the Directors and Canadians for their role in Afghanistan. It was a touching moment giving credibility and credence to the Museum and its thoughtful exhibits.

I was impressed to see that once complete, CMHR will cover almost every human rights atrocity that I can remember in my lifetime and perhaps to the beginning of the century.

On level 2, they begin with an experience called "What are Human Rights" and work their way through "Indigenous Perspectives" to "Canadian Journeys". Indigenous Perspectives is considered the most dramatic spaces of the Museum consisting of a circular theater of curved wooden slats representing the multitude of Aboriginal traditions.

On level 3 there is an exhibit about Protecting Rights in Canada which deals with the legal aspects of human rights. A "living tree" projection evokes the constant growth of laws and social change while through a digitally interfaced debate table visitors can explore legal cases and give their own opinion.

On level 4 is the Holocaust gallery where 'broken glass' theater examines Canada's own experiences with antisemitism along with and exhibit called "Breaking the Silence" and "Turning Points for Humanity".

On Level 5 we examine "Rights Today" dealing with contemporary human rights struggles through an interactive wall map. Level 6 deals with Expressions, a gallery that will feature a range of temporary exhibits and Level 7 is about Inspiring positive social change, inviting visitors to contemplate their own role in building human rights for a better world.

Most of the exhibits are digitally interactive and I was impressed to see that there is a digital learning table where one can study and explore up to 80 human rights tragedies of the world including Residential Schools, the Pakistan/India partition, Palestine and other causes.

I came away a proud Canadian for the opportunity to visit The Canadian Museum for Human Rights and thinking that perhaps Canadians like controversy because I saw no cause for it.

A Birthday Reborn

January 21, which is my birthday, will never be the same for me ever again. In 2016 on this date which is always a celebration, I found myself in Stockholm, Sweden for a series of conferences and seminars.

I was invited by an organization called GAPF which is essentially a commemoration for the memory of two Swedish girls Pela and Fadime. I had no idea who these girls were and it was a shock to hear their heart-rending stories. It was also a very important wake up call. January 21, 2002 was the date on which Fadime Sahindal was killed by her father and I will always commemorate her memory on this day. Why? Because Fadime is a symbol for the thousands of girls who are murdered in the name of honour all over the world but who we easily forget.

However thanks to the persistent and inspirational work of a Swedish woman of Kurdish heritage, Sara Mohammad, today everyone on the streets of Sweden knows the name Fadime.

Fadime Şahindal was opposed to her family's insistence on an arranged marriage, and instead selected her own boyfriend. At first she kept the relationship secret, but her father found out about it. Fadime then left her family and moved to Sundsvall, where her brother found her and threatened her. She went to the police who advised her at first to talk to her family. She then turned to the media with her story, after which she turned again to the police and was offered a secret identity. By turning to the media Fadime managed to receive support from the Swedish authorities, but she had also made the "shame" of her family public. She filed a lawsuit against her father and brother, accusing them of unlawful threats, and won.

Fadime was scheduled to move in with her boyfriend, Patrick, the following month, in June 1998, when he died in a car accident. He was buried in Uppsala.

Her father forbade her to visit Uppsala, since he did not want her to visit her deceased boyfriend's grave. Nalin Pekgul, a Kurdish-Swedish parliamentarian, negotiated a compromise in which Şahindal agreed to stay away from Uppsala and her father promised not to stalk her.

On 20 November 2001, the Violence Against Women network arranged a seminar on the topic "Integration on whose terms?". During the seminar Fadime spoke in front of the Riksdag (Swedish Parliament) about her personal story.

On 21 January 2002, Fadime secretly visited her mother and sisters in Uppsala. During the visit, her father arrived and shot her in the head in front of her mother and two sisters. Confronted by police, he confessed and said to his defense that he was ill. Despite the confession, one of her cousins later tried to convince the police that he had killed her.

Her father was ultimately convicted of murder by a Swedish court and sentenced to life imprisonment.

Her murder sparked a debate in Sweden about immigrant integration and raised questions regarding Patrick's death.

Fadime was buried in Uppsala.

Pela Atroshi's murder in Dohuk, in Iraqi Kurdistan, was officially deemed an honour killing by both Iraqi and Swedish authorities. Pela was an intelligent and good-looking girl. When she emigrated with her family to Sweden in 1995, she took to Swedish ways—eventually leaving the family home in January 1999.

But after a time she missed her parents and six younger brothers and sisters and returned, agreeing to an arranged marriage in Kurdistan. It was a front—the men in her family had decided to kill her in their home town of Dohuk, northern Iraq, where honour killings were considered minor crimes, and where the Atroshi clan commanded immense respect.

Since Fadime and Pela's murders, GAPF headed by Sara Mohammad and many Kurdish-Swedish volunteers have been lobbying to make Honor Based Violence a criminal offence and have a specific separate listing in the penal code for HBV. The work done by GAPF has resulted in the entire country becoming aware of the threat of honour killings for many more girls and women. Two men have also been murdered in Honour killings in Sweden so it's not only women who are the victims of this barbaric practice.

GAPF has now made the month of January a month of commemoration for Fadime. I was invited to attend part of these events.

On January 19 I went to Västerås where there was a screening of Honor Diaries followed by Q & A. At every event local politicians and media were invited so that the murder could stay alive in the minds of people.

On January 20 there was a full day conference held at the Swedish Parliament in collaboration with political parties and 81 other organizations. Honor Diaries was screened to a room full of politicians from every party, law makers and the public. This was a very well organized event with open discussion and raw questions asked. GAPF put the politicians and law makers on the spot and recalled Fadime's words when she had pleaded to Parliament to take note of what is happening to her and other girls. I spoke from the perspective on Canada.

On January 21, we had a very poignant and emotional day which we spent in Uppsala, which was where Fadime is buried. A park in Uppsala has been dedicated to Fadime. On a day where the weather was minus 20 and freezing beyond description, Sara Mohammad and her volunteers lit torches in the park and spoke about Fadime's life. From there we went to the graveyard and laid wreaths on her grave and spoke at length about the importance of keeping her memory alive.

Then we went to the school where Fadime had studied and spoke to the students. A room at the school is now dedicated to Fadime where students are invited to come for discussion and debate.

At every event, including the outdoors, Fadime's favorite song is played by live musicians or recorded.

All this is to say that nowhere else in the world do I see a commitment like I saw in Sweden. The Kurdish-Swedish women I met are firebrands and activists who do not stop at anything despite threats from the Islamists to hold back their words and their work. I have never met a person like Sara Mohammad who spends 18 to 20 hours a day on this work where she has dedicated her life to keeping Fadime's memory alive. She has certainly succeeded in making me aware that we need to do the same in Canada.

The Ultimate Journey to the Center of Our Faiths

The month of December holds a special meaning for our family. Twenty years ago, we landed at Toronto airport on a snowy, wintry, freezing December night. Alone, scared and cold, we were welcomed by the warmth of Christmas cheer so this time of the year is very poignant. This year December heralds Eid, Hanukkah and Christmas so we wanted to do something special to celebrate 2 decades of living in this multi-faith mosaic we call home.

For many years, especially after having performed the Haj we had a passionate desire to visit Jerusalem. For me, it became all the more urgent because in my interfaith work, I used to speak about Judaism, Christianity and Islam being from the same source and that despite our differences and challenges, we are the children of Abraham. That is for believers of course.

As well, I believe that when we ask, God answers so all of sudden there was a window of opportunity to visit Jerusalem. We were thrilled but there was no time to prepare in detail. I shot off quick emails to all my Jewish friends and each one came back with ideas, suggestions and contacts. (BTW this trip was a personal and spiritual journey funded by us with no political agenda other than to refresh and revive our weary souls!).

We decided that a visit to the Holy Land must be shared with those who have similar dreams. So we invited our dear friends Jim Evans, a United Church Minister and his wife Karen to come along and I can say in retrospect, that their presence made this trip far richer than we expected.

There was caution and concern. People who had traveled previously told us that there is a lot of security and red tape and we must be prepared to wait at the airport for hours. Well, when one goes on a spiritual journey, doors open in amazing ways. We took a direct flight to Tel Aviv and were out of the airport in less than 10 minutes!

Tel Aviv is a vibrant, bustling metropolis on the shores of the Mediterranean, full of international tourists and beautiful hotels.

Hope in Haifa

In Tel Aviv we were met by our companion and guide for the visit—Sam an Orthodox Jew from Montreal. Our friends stopped of at Caesarea, while we went to Haifa where the University had invited us to come for a visit to the only Jewish Arab Center there. It was inspiring to see Jewish and Arab students working, walking, talking, sharing and eating side by side. Dr. Faisal Azaiza, who heads the JAC welcomed us and showed us the campus. He shared with us the various programs to try and build peace and have conflict resolution between the two communities. I was particularly impressed by the program on Women's Empowerment and noted that the library housed more books on Islam and Women, than anywhere I've seen so far. The University addresses issues beyond the fluff stuff i.e. models for co-existence, conflict resolution, economic disparity, bilingualism and more grass roots concerns like social interaction.

Physically Haifa is a beautiful city with the largest Baha'i Temple perched on a hill with hanging gardens. We were recommended to stay at the Haddad guesthouse on the main street and it turned out that the owner's cousin works in Air Canada! We stayed overnight enjoying the food in outdoor café's—the coffee was an aroma I've never tasted before and the Mediterranean cuisine yumlicious.

Spiritually, many important events in the life of the Prophet Elijah (9th century BC) are said to have happened in a revered cave in Haifa. The cave is sacred to Jews, Christians, Muslims, and Druze, all of whom venerate the prophet Elijah. There was a mosque here until 1948. Tradition also has it that the Holy Family (Mary, Joseph and Jesus) found shelter in this cave for a night on their return from Egypt. We were also told that Prophet Elijah ascended to the skies from this cave. It was interesting to note that all three traditions have faith in some form of ascension and all of them took place in the Holy Land.

Jerusalem—The Sacred City

When God created beauty, he created 10 parts of it and gave 9 to Jerusalem. He created knowledge and did the same and the same thing when He created suffering. Ancient Hebrew saying.

From Haifa we took a bus to Jerusalem because there is such beauty on the way. I could see small villages dotted with minarets, olive groves and gardens of fruit. Traveling towards Jerusalem was a moving experience because we felt we were going back in time to experience moments of miracles, sacrifice and tolerance (something we seem to have forgotten today), and our first view of the old city was heartwarming. Our friends had fortuitously arranged for our stay at a Scottish Church guest house overlooking the walled city. From our room we could see the Dome of the Rock and it was an incredible synergy. We understood why the city of Jerusalem is known in Arabic as Al-Quds or Baitul-Maqadis ("The Noble, Sacred Place"). Jerusalem is perhaps the only city in the world that is considered historically and spiritually significant to all three monotheistic faiths.

The Temple Mount is the holiest site in Judaism. According to the Bible, the Talmud, and other sources of Jewish tradition, several important events in the history of Judaism took place on the Temple Mount. Here God gathered the earth from which he formed Adam. Here Adam, Cain, Abel and Noah offered sacrifices to God. Here Abraham passed God's test by showing his willingness to sacrifice his son Isaac. Here Jacob dreamt about angels ascending and descending a ladder while sleeping on a stone (the stone in the Dome of the Rock is believed to be the very stone). Here King Solomon built the Temple in 950 BC, which stood for 410 years until King Nebuchadnezzar destroyed it in 586 BC. Here the Second Temple was built after the Babylonian Exile, which was destroyed by the Romans in 70 AD. During Maimonides' residence in Jerusalem, a synagogue stood on the Temple Mount alongside other structures and Maimonides prayed there.

For Christians, it is the site of Christ's crucifixion, burial and resurrection The Temple Mount is believed to contain the "pinnacle of the Temple" from which Satan tempted Jesus to jump to prove his status as the Messiah (near Al Aqsa Mosque). The courtyard by the mosques provides an excellent view of surrounding Christian sites, including the Dome of the Ascension (marking the site from which where Jesus ascended into heaven) and the church of Dominus Flevit (commemorating the spot where Jesus wept as he saw a vision of Jerusalem in ruins).

For Muslims it is important because Muhammad originally established Jerusalem as the qibla (direction of prayer) before changing it to Mecca. As well Islam respects Abraham, David and Solomon as prophets, and regards the Temple as one of the earliest and most noteworthy places of worship of God. Verse 17:1 of the Qur'an speaks of the Prophet's night journey to the "farthest Mosque" (al-masjid al-Aqsa). This is traditionally interpreted to be the site at the Temple Mount in Jerusalem on which the mosque of that name now stands.

Jim and Karen had already toured the area and since it was close to sunset, they suggested we could go to the masjid to pray. They took us directly to the Chain gate where we could go to Masjid al Aqsa. Our path took us by the Western Wall and it was amazing that what we had seen only on TV, was now a reality. It was in the courtyard here that we saw observant Jews hurrying to pray at the wall, religious Muslim going to the masjid and practicing Christians going to see their sacred spaces—each one careful not to step on each other's toes. It was incredible to note that Catholic, Jewish and Muslim women all covered themselves and it was completely natural. The diversity was interesting and insightful.

The first sight of Dome of the Rock and Masjid al Aqsa was like a dream come true. We had been literally dreaming of praying at Al-Aqsa for many months now and here we were with our souls melted in the form of tears rolling down our faces unashamedly as we stood in humility and awe in front of our first Qibla. Inside the Dome we touched the Rock which is as big as a room. Steps leading to a room under the Rock, took us to a tiny chamber where it's believed that Prophet Mohammad prayed with other Prophets including Abraham. The entire room is soaked in fragrance and we wanted to just sit there and reflect on this miracle of God.

Fact that our Christian friends guided us to our places of worship is no surprise and suddenly my visions of seeing crosses for the past two years, became a reality. We were meant to come here with our Christian Brother and sister and feel the connection.

A young lad attached himself to us as a guide and took us to the key spots at the Haram es Shariff where there were schools, libraries, the spot where Buraq was tethered and fountains. I think what hit me most was how little we know of our history but of course as with all history, there are many versions. Here is what we understood.

History and Emotions

Dome of the Rock (Qubbat as-Sakhrah) can be seen from all over Jerusalem. It is the crowning glory of the Haram es-Sharif ("Noble Sanctuary"), or Temple Mount. The Dome of the Rock is not a mosque, but a Muslim shrine. Like the Ka'ba in Mecca, it is built over a sacred stone. This stone is believed to be the place from which the Prophet Muhammad ascended into heaven during his Night Journey to heaven. The Dome of the Rock is the oldest Islamic monument that stands today and certainly one of the most beautiful. It also boasts the oldest surviving mihrab (niche indicating the direction of Mecca) in the world. By the 11th century, several legends had developed concerning the Dome of the Rock and its sacred stone, including the following:

They say that on the night of his Ascension into Heaven the Prophet, peace and blessing be upon him, prayed first at the Dome of the Rock, laying his hand upon the Rock. As he went out, the Rock, to do him honor, rose up, but he laid his hand on it to keep it in its place and firmly fixed it there. But by reason of this rising up, it is even to this present day partly detached from the ground beneath.

In the Middle Ages, Christians and Muslims both believed the dome to be the biblical Temple of Solomon. The Knights Templar made their headquarters there during the Crusades and later patterned their churches after its design.

The exterior mosaics that once adorned the Dome of the Rock suffered from exposure to Jerusalem winters. They were repaired in the Mamluk period, and then completely replaced with tiles by Sulieman the Magnificent in 1545. At the same time, he created the parapet wall with its intricate inscription by filling up the thirteen small arches that originally topped each facade. The windows of the Dome of the Rock date from this period as well. The tiling was completely replaced in the last major restoration in 1956-62.

The Al-Aqsa Mosque (Arabic Masjid Al-Aqsa, "Distant Mosque"—is part of the complex of religious buildings known as the Haram esh-Sharif (the Noble Sanctuary) to Muslims and the Temple Mount to Jews, and is the third holiest site in Islam, after Mecca and Medina. The first Al-Aqsa Mosque was constructed of wood by the Umayyads in 710 AD, only a few decades after the Dome of the Rock. The structure has been rebuilt at least five times; it was entirely destroyed at least once by earthquakes. The last major rebuild was in 1035. When the Crusaders captured Jerusalem in 1099, Al-Aqsa became the headquarters of the Templars. Their legacy remains in the three central bays of the main facade. In the mid-14th century the Mamelukes added an extra two on either side, resulting in the seven bays that stand today.

Currently, the Temple Mount / Haram Es Sharif is governed by the Waqf, the Supreme Muslim Religious Council. The site has been under Muslim control since the Muslim reconquest of the crusader Kingdom of Jerusalem in the 12th century.

Needless to say, we visited the Harem ash Shariif as often as we could during our stay in Al-Quds but more importantly, we were able to visit other holy sites with Jim and Karen who became our spiritual guides because they had done extensive homework and had books of history which we learnt from. Our biggest surprise and delight was that every step we took showed us the incredible bonds that link us together with our brothers and sisters in creation.

Visiting the Christian Sites with Our Companions

The Church of the Holy Sepulcher has been an important pilgrimage destination since the 4th century, and it remains the holiest Christian site in the world. It stands on a site that is believed to house the tomb and burial slab where Jesus' body was placed before his resurrection.

In my interfaith dialogue, there is a story I tell my audience about when Jerusalem was conquered by Muslims. Omar came to the Church of the Holy Sepulcher which is a revered Christian site and it was time to pray. The patriarch offered the church but Omar said no. If he prayed there, Muslims might one day build a mosque so he went and prayed across the street. Today there is a Mosque of Omar in that spot across the street.

We went with Jim and Karen inside the church where you can feel the agony of Mary as she stood on the stairs and watched her son's body being anointed on a slab. The walls of the sanctuary tell the heartrending story and I could sense the sadness. It's powerful and moving and everywhere we went, there was light—even in the darkness. We lit candles for all the people we know who would be there but could not—yet. Then we went across the street to the masjid and prayed there with Jim and Karen. The realization that we are connected is very strong for those who can sense the fragile ties that bind us together.

We were told that fierce disputes, lasting centuries, between Christian creeds over ownership of the church were largely resolved by an Ottoman decree issued in 1852. Still in force and known as the Status Quo, it divides custody among Armenians, Greeks, Copts, Roman Catholics, Ethiopians and Syrians. Some areas are administered communally. Every day, the church is unlocked by a Muslim keyholder acting as a "neutral" intermediary. This ceremonial task has been performed by a member of the same family for several generations and Jim and Karen woke up at 4am to witness this ceremony.

We walked to the Mount of Olives which has many sacred sites. To add to our amazement, the place where Jesus is believed to have ascended to the heavens is inside a mosque. The Chapel of the Ascension on Mount of Olives is a Christian and Muslim holy site that is believed to mark the place where Jesus ascended into heaven. The small round church/mosque contains a stone imprinted with the footprints of Jesus. Outside the Chapel is an unmarked tomb believed by many to be the grave of Rabia al-Adawiyya, the first Sufi saint of Islam. We were blessed and honored to offer a prayer there.

The Garden of Gethsemane is at the foot of the Mount of Olives, within the walled grounds of the Church of all Nations (also known as the Church of the Agony). It's a peaceful garden among a grove of ancient olive trees, looking back at the eastern wall of the City of Jerusalem. A modern Franciscan church marks the spot where Jesus wept over his vision of the future destruction of Jerusalem. There are 12 Olive trees and a stone statue of Jesus weeping which would turn the hardest heart to tears. The number 12—as in 12 disciples and the belief in 12 Imams is not a co-incidence. In addition, Caliph Umar prayed at Gethsemane in 638.

We then visited the Church of Mary Magdalene which has stunning gold domes, Church of John the Baptist and the Convent of the Pater Noster where it is believed Jesus taught The Lords Prayer. This is a serene green sanctuary where the Lords prayer is listed in 60 languages on huge tiled walls. Having learnt The Lords Prayer in convent school and being a fervent supporter of it in Canada, I was moved by the spot. We also prayed at The Tombs of the Prophets which is a site on the Mount of Olives that a medieval Jewish tradition identifies as the tombs of the prophets Haggai, Zechariah, and Malachi, who lived in the 6th-5th centuries BC. Both Jews and Christians venerate the site as the tombs of these prophets of the last three books of the Old Testament.

From Mount of Olives we saw the Gate of Mercy, the Gate of Gold, the Gate of Eternal Life, Sha'ar Harahamim. This appears in the legends of all three religions. An early Jewish tradition holds that it is through that gate that the Messiah will enter Jerusalem. According to Christian tradition, Jesus made his last entry to Jerusalem through the Mercy Gate. The Muslims refer to it as the Gate of Mercy and believe it to be the gate referred to in the Koran, through which the just will pass on the Day of Judgment.

At the base of the Mount of Olives is a church said to mark the Tomb of the Virgin Mary, the mother of Jesus. Centered around a quarried-out tomb that may well date from the 1st century, the Tomb of the Virgin is venerated by Muslims because, during his Night Journey from Mecca to Jerusalem, the Prophet Muhammad saw a light over Mary's tomb. Our tears flowed freely and with no hesitation because this is a place where you can feel the blessed presence of a revered mother.

The Jewish Quarter—An Education

One of the most delightful parts of the visit was walking the cobbled stone streets of the Jewish quarter and seeing some of the most unusual architecture. We stopped for coffee and an authentic bagel and went to the Burnt house. We visited the Wohl Archeological Museum which is extremely educational. Located under a modern Jewish seminary in the Jewish Quarter, the Museum contains remains of Jewish dwellings from the era of Herod the Great (37-4 BC). In the time of Herod, the area of the modern-day Jewish Quarter was was part of a luxurious "Upper City," occupied primarily by the families of important Jewish Temple priests. Excavations after the 1967 war exposed the remains of several mansions dating to this period. This rediscovered Herodian quarter now lies from 3 to 7 meters below street level, preserved in the Wohl Archaeological Museum. It's mind boggling how the intricate work has been done so effectively. The Tomb of David is a much-revered site on Mount Zion in Jerusalem that has been variously owned and jealously guarded by Christians, Muslims and Jews throughout its history. Today it is a Jewish holy site.

The Citadel of Jerusalem is better known as the Tower of David. Nowadays the fort is distinguished by its Islamic towers and entrance porch, but the Citadel's history goes back way before that. The Jewish historian Josephus first called the fortress the "Citadel of King David." The name "David's Tower" now refers to the minaret on the South side. To make things confusing the term "David's Tower" used to be reserved in the past for the north-east tower, whose origin is Herodian.

From the Sublime to the Souq

A visit to Jerusalem is not complete or possible without marketing at the souq. The winding cobbled stone streets of the inner city are a shop-a-holics delight! Jim and I soon discovered that our spouses are serious shoppers but there was only one haggler amongst all of us— Sohail. After the three of us naïve in our Canadian ways had paid the asked-for price more than once, Sohail jumped into the fray with full attention. We stood outside the shop while the bargaining built up for hand carved olive wood pieces. The Arab shopkeepers didn't know what hit them with this experienced Pakistani shopper who's just returned from China! Voices got louder and reinforcements were called in. At one point Jim and Karen looked like they were going to run away and asked me if Sohail and the shopkeepers might come to blows! Hah I said—just watch. It's only just begun. So we sat and were offered tea and juice and we waited. Sohail came out to smoke a cigar for strength but by this time, they were calling each other "brother". Good sign. Bad sign when we threatened to go to the next shop and discovered that they were all related. I'm used to this but Jim and Karen were wide eyed and a bit concerned until they saw that the bill was down to one fourth the original price. They never stepped inside a shop the entire trip without the amazing haggler. One souvenir that speaks to my heart is the palm of the hand called "khamsa" which is considered by everyone there to be the protective hand of God supported by an eye to ward off evil.

The West Bank and Bethlehem

A friend's daughter who lives in Bethlehem came to pick us up and took us on a tour of the West Bank and her home. While we were in the rest of Israel, we saw progress, education and wealth. In Bethlehem we saw knowledge, beauty and pain intertwined in the writings on the wall that divides the two communities. Bethlehem is the birth place of Jesus which is a thing of beauty. There is great knowledge in the history of the cobbled streets and in the minds and hearts of the Palestinian elders sitting on the corner café sipping coffee. One old man has sat there for 20 years sharing his wisdom. We understood their passionate need for a homeland and at the same time, the desire to be recognized.

We've come back from the Holy Land with renewed respect and admiration for both sides, realizing that there is a turbulent history of the past and present here, but also with a sense that there is hope for peace if there is a desire to make it happen.

I have heard that many eons ago Jerusalem was considered to the fountain of wisdom because of the shared knowledge of our three traditions. I hope and pray that we will one day learn to share that knowledge again, and use it for peace with each other.

Women of Faith Build Hope and Homes

> *The most effective way to do it, is to do it.*
> *Amelia Earhart*

When Judy Csillag, Director Community Outreach and Partnerships for The Canadian Centre for Diversity asked me if I would like to participate in a Women of Faith build for Habitat for Humanity, I said yes with no idea of what this would entail. Little did I know that this would turn out to be one of the most meaningful and unusual experiences of my life.

Since I came to Canada twenty years ago, there has always been an urge to give back to this wonderful country that is my adopted land and that has given me and my family a roof over our heads, jobs, security and most of all freedom. I realize that many people don't have these luxuries in their native lands or take them for granted in Canada. So I volunteer wherever I can but the Habitat experience takes volunteering to a whole new level. Habitat has a vision for a world where everyone has a safe and decent place to live. Their mission is to mobilize volunteers and community partners in building affordable housing and promoting homeownership as a means to breaking the cycle of poverty. To uphold the dignity of every human being, Habitat works with partnerships and a belief of faith in action.

The mission of The Canadian Centre for Diversity is to build bridges between communities and to build a society that celebrates diversity, difference, and inclusion so it's no wonder that with Habitat, they came up with the idea of a Women of Faith build. Co-Chairs of the project were Rabbi Lori Cohen, Reverend Cathy Gibbs and Tanya Khan. It was a smooth, well planned and well executed project. Thirty women from six faith communities were invited to participate and we met at the Bishop Strachan School for our mandatory training session. But it was not just training. Thanks to the insight of The Canadian Centre for Diversity and Habitat, we got to know each other through various interactions. The energy was amazing and all the women who were there came with a passion for building bridges—not only cement ones but those of the heart and mind. This is when my own interfaith work was truly validated. We were given instructions, directions, enthusiasm, inspiration and a little pink hammer pin! We were women from Sikh, Muslim, Christian, Jewish, Hindu and Aboriginal traditions who shared our vision to come together to build homes for those in need.

Bright and early on October 16, I got up feeling like this was going to be a special day. Special it was because it started out with clouds in the sky and then I guess prayers went up from at least six faith traditions and the heavens opened up to smile with the sun. The location for our build was on Kingston Road and we got there sharp on time. At the site we were welcomed by a real crew, members from Habitat for Humanity Toronto, The Canadian Centre for Diversity, our co-chairs, some media and coffee. We got our instructions, a T-shirt saying Women of Faith Build 2008, hard hats with our names on them, steel toed boots and gloves. I've never worn a hardhat and boots so I clunked around feeling like I was going to fall (for some of the more petite women, sizes were a challenge because the shoes belonged to the male workers but they made it work by wearing double socks and sometimes mismatched shoes like moi). We were divided in groups of 5 with a leader who from the core building team. We started by standing in a circle while Valerie John from Toronto Council Fire Native Cultural Centre began the day with a smudge ceremony and a universal prayer for peace and off we went. The spirit and enthusiasm was infectious.

At the site, there were five half-finished apartments and our mission was to build the back walls. "Yikes" I thought "I've never built anything let alone held a real hammer", but like the others, I was raring to go. We were told we have two coffee breaks and lunch (more than some women get at work!) so off we went following our leaders. The site is quite hazardous if one is not careful because there are beams, wood, equipment all over the place. Mike our group leader was an older experienced worker and he patiently guided us. Our project was carry heavy drywall to the room, measure, cut and paste a plastic vapor barrier over the basic wall and put a dirty black glue on it. (Dirty, because if it gets on anything, you can't get it off. I was glad I wore a black sweat shirt.) On top of that we had to put drywall and drill it in with nails. Sounds easy but cutting drywall to fit around corners is a challenge. I thought using a drill would be a cinch—not! It takes a steady hand and lots of pressure. If Mike has not guided us, we would have made serious mistakes. I developed a whole new respect for the men who do this work daily.

Now being women, there was a lot of chitter-chatter and we would wander off to see what was happening at the next lot. Some were younger and faster than others. There was a lot of sharing and compassion i.e. when I could not carry heavy stuff, others pitched in. We shared, cared, laughed, worked, exchanged recipes, spoke of our kids and took a break when we were exhausted. But it was one of the most inspiring moments in my life when the first wall was completed. Our communal cry of "Oyeh" was heard all over Kingston Road. People walking by stopped to see this motley crew of women working so hard for a common cause for humanity. It was amusing to see the new fashion statement by women in hijab wearing a hard hat—it was much more comfortable than ours because the hijab acted as a lining. My hard hat kept falling off but one woman told me to wear it backwards and it worked.

At breaks we exchanged notes. A warm vegetarian lunch was provided by Grace Church-on-the-Hill. I went to grab a coffee at the corner coffee shop and the owners were totally impressed by the work we were doing. In our group were three young (17 years old) students from CHAT—Community Hebrew Academy of Toronto. Mira, Danielle and Shira said "it's an awesome experience to meet all these women". For most of the women, the cause was inspiring because we had done some fund raising to get here, but more importantly it was the interaction with diverse women that made their day so meaningful. Helen Warner, Public Affairs Director for Church of Latter Day Saints said "I find we have so much more in common than what separates us. Along with homes, we are building relationships."

Naheed Khokhar from the Ahmaddiya community felt elated at what she called "a brilliant experience" while Valerie John from Council Fire expressed "this is the first time I'm doing something like this. It's so poignant because it affects a real family so our work will live with them for as long as they reside in this house—it's a generational thing." On generations, many women were interested in bringing their youth for a build and we were told it's easy. They must be over 16, and ready to work one day from 08:30 to 4:30 (although I must boast that as women, we finished early!)

Barbara Wilson, family outreach coordinator for Habitat informed me that most of the work at Habitat for Humanity is volunteer and 60% of volunteers are women. Sally Wasserman, an energetic eightysomething Holocaust survivor, said "it's absolutely wonderful to be part of a community build. If I can contribute even one nail it's worthwhile specially meeting all these wonderful women who I would not have met otherwise". I noted emails and cards being exchanged, women giving each high fives and hugs. Gurwinder Gill who is Director Diversity Services for William Osler Health Centre this was an experience of cultural diversity where women crossed all boundaries of faith and culture putting aside biases in working together for a cause that touched all of them. "It makes me optimistic that if there is a will, we can move towards peace."

I prayed for change,
so I changed my mind.

I prayed for guidance
and learned to trust myself.

I prayed for happiness
and realized I am not my ego.

*I prayed for peace
and learned to accept others unconditionally.*

*I prayed for abundance
and realized my doubt kept it out.*

*I prayed for wealth
and realized it is my health.*

*I prayed for a miracle
and realized I am the miracle.*

*I prayed for a soul mate
and realized I am the One.*

*I prayed for love
and realized it's always knocking,*

but I have to allow it in.

Rumi

Finding Spirituality in India

> *Agar firdaus bar roo-e zameen ast,*
> *Hameen ast-o hameen ast-o hameen ast*
> *If there is a paradise on earth,*
> *It is this, it is this, it is this (India).*
>
> **Hazrat Amir Khusrau**

2007 is the year in which I quit my fulltime job to pursue some higher learning and knowledge. I yearned to travel somewhere where my soul would be nourished. I waited and when the invitation came, it was from a most unexpected source. WISCOMP, an organization of women in Delhi, India working towards peace and conflict resolution invited me to a workshop at the end of December. I thought I would never be able to go because my passport was expiring, it was a time of the year when travel is impossible and I would never get an Indian visa in time. However at the back of my mind was the thought—"Delhi, the city of Dergahs where my parents grew up near Karolbagh, Delhi of Qutub Minar where the smallest Masjid in the grounds was built by my grandfather and the proximity to Ajmer where my soul can be renewed—I must go"

I believe that when the 'calling' (bullawa) is there, no one can stop destiny from working in a positive force. Within one week I got my passport renewed and arrived at the Indian consulate where a compassionate and kind Consul General gave me a tourist visa in two days (usually unheard of). My ticket to travel was arranged so smoothly that one would never believe end of December is peak season. Friends in Toronto gave me contacts and phone numbers in Delhi. Armed with nothing but my desire to seek spirituality, I arrived at Delhi airport on the morning of December 9, to the sound of chaiwallas, (tea makers) rickshaws, chirping birds and mooing cows. It felt like coming home. This was my third trip to Delhi but my first with a purpose of renewing my spirit. From day one, everything was perfectly orchestrated for me by a power bigger than all of us. I asked no questions because I felt a gentle hand at my back. I just said shukria (thanks) and kept my head bowed in humility.

I stayed at the India Islamic Cultural Centre which is next to Lodhi Gardens where I would go and sit to contemplate how I got there. IICC was like an Indian "Fawlty Towers" with Muslim overtones. One phone, the internet worked maybe one hour a day but I was so disconnected with technology that it was a blessing. It was central and clean, and most importantly it was humble. This trip was not about 5 star hotels—it was important to stay rooted close the ground. Besides, who could complain— I got strong mixed chai around the clock! The building is grand with beautiful calligraphy, manicured gardens, two auditoriums and Dilli Darbar (a Mughlai restaurant). I was immediately impressed because they had a huge Christmas tree in the front lawn because they celebrate the pluralism of India. It was across the street from Habitat which is the hub of arts in Delhi, and next to the India Cultural Centre which was the venue of our workshops.

On Thursday I reconnected with Peachy, my childhood friend who I had lost touch with. Being a sufi at heart, she took me to the Dargah of Hazrat Amir Khusrau and Nizamuddin Auliya through the back lanes which no one knows. It was a moonlit night, and as we arrived the Sama was just beginning. Soon the strains of Mun Kunto Maula filled the night air as we inhaled ittar, agar batti (incense) and something indefinable in that night air. It was the perfume of roses, loved by our Prophet (pbuh) and musk. I was able to buy authentic Amir Khusrau music (not the commercial pop stuff). Here you see humanity at its lowest ebb and at its highest but there is no barrier between rich and poor, between Hindu, Muslim and Sikh as the only people who come there are those seeking spiritual comfort.

A bit about Amir Khusrau

Amir Khusrau Dehlavi (1253-1325 AD), a prolific Persian poet associated with royal courts of more than seven rulers of Delhi Sultanate, is also popular in much of North India and Pakistan, through many playful riddles, songs and legends attributed to him. Through his enormous literary output and the legendary folk personality, Khusrau represents one of the first (recorded) Indian personages with a true multi-cultural or pluralistic identity.

The tradition says that one first pays respect to Hazrat Amir Khusrau as he was the student of Hazrat Nizamuddin Auliya. So we bought flowers and incense and did our hazari. A bit about Hazrat Nizamuddin Auliya.

Hazrat Khawaja Nizamuddin Auliya, also known as Hazrat Nizamuddin, was a famous Sufisaint of the Chishti Order in India. He was born in Badayun (east of Delhi), though he later settled in Delhi, where his shrine (Nizamuddin Dargah) is still located. His original name was Mohammed. He was also the spiritual master of Amir Khusro.

The following is a translation of Hazrat Nizamuddin Awlia's famous poem in honour of the Prophet:

O breeze! turn towards Medina
and from this well-wisher recite the Salaam.

Turn round the king of the prophets
and with the utmost humility recite the Salaam.

Sometimes pass the gate of mercy
and with the gate of Gabriel rule the forehead.

Salaam to the prophet of God
and sometimes recite Salaam at the gate of peace.

Put with all respect the head of faith on the dust there.

Be one with the sweet melody of David
and be acquainted with the cry of anguish.

In the assembly of the prophets recite verses from the humble being.

That night I slept with the fragrance of roses around me enveloped in a warmth hard to describe. Next morning I saw a poster about an event at the Habitat center called RUMI—UNVEIL THE SUN. This was a play being performed to a select audience by invitation only. Being an eternal optimist, I arrived at the venue and who is standing at the door but Suhaila Kapoor (sister of Shekhar Kapoor) director of the play and someone I had met in Toronto. She gave me a pass for the play and I spent an evening enthralled at how a totally non-Muslim cast and crew captured the spirit of Rumi, complete with poetry, music, and whirling. The director Amrit Kent writes:

"My search for Rumi began years ago. Sufism is part of my Punjabi heritage and as a singer I sang sufiana kalam for many years. I have also written a stage script on Punjab's pre-eminent Sufi poet, Baba Bulle Shah. It was inevitable that my quest would lead to Jalaluddin Rumi. As I immersed myself deeper in Sufi thought, what struck me most was the secular nature of Sufi mysticism that leaves no room for prejudice about religion, race or caste. All is One'.

"Such a vision is sorely needed to heal today's increasingly violent and divided world." Amrit Kent

The play was beautifully performed with authentic music. As I was leaving, an unknown benefactor, a kind patron gifted me a CD of the music. Next day the workshops started and I met 50 young professionals from India and Pakistan as well as Kashmir. This is part of the report I did on the workshops.

On Day 2 of the workshop one young girl from Pakistan asked me if my mother's name was Salma and if I had ever lived in Sialkot? Yes I said shocked. It turns out her mother was in school with me more than 30 years ago! The young lady attached herself to me for the entire duration of the conference. I will never forget the wonderfully talented and warm people I met.

During the workshops I was stressing about how to get to Ajmer. People said I shouldn't go alone but a young girl Priyanka, said she is from Ajmer and will arrange everything. Meanwhile my Sikh friend Sohini who lives in Delhi said she's always wanted to go to Ajmer so she would come with me. I was delighted. Workshops ended on Thursday 18 and I knew Eid was Friday 19 December in India. Priyanka booked us tickets on the Shitabdi which is the fast train to Ajmer. We left at 6am in a train full of pilgrims going to Ajmer—most of them Hindus and Sikhs. The train was air conditioned, clean and they served us amazing food in biodegradable containers. Sohini and I were contemplating the easiest way to go the Dargah and we had agreed that we would get a taxi and a guide since neither one of us knew where we were going and we had only two hours in which to do the hazari (visit). The train was late and as we stepped on to the platform, a gentleman with rosy cheeks and a curled moustache stepped up to me and said "are you Raheel Raza?" To say I was shocked is an understatement. I said yes but how did you know? You must have seen a photo. He said no. He was Priyanka's dad, an army colonel who had taken the day off work to come and receive us. He had a jeep and driver ready and told us that due to lack of time, we must do as he says. We followed him as he flashed his ID and rushed us through the bazaar which was packed with men, women, children, animals, vendors, slippers and everything else under the sun. Do you think we even noticed that we were walking barefoot through the streets of Ajmer? I remember Ammie always praying to Allah to introduce us to good people and that time I knew what she had meant. People had appeared as angels throughout this trip and I could not thank God enough. Colonel Singh wrapped a white handkerchief around his head, found us a guide (he knew everyone there) and took us to the Dargah. He helped us get flowers and a chaddar (shett of flowers) and tabbaruk (sweets). Tears ran down my face and the khadim (custodian) of the Dargah said "sit down—we will do dua" I wanted to pray there. He cleared a space for me and I performed nafal (prayers). Then he asked me for names of people who wanted dua (prayer) in their name and wrote then in a register and read a dua for us. We were in a daze and a dream. We also took a tour of the Dargah and saw the huge deghs (large cooking vessels) in which food is cooked and distributed to the poor. Colonel Singh himself did all the rituals with great aqeedat (sincerity). It was ironical. Here I was with two Sikhs at the Dargah of Khwaja Ghareeb Nawaz! Such is the connection of the Sufis.

Dargah Shariff of Hazrat Khwaja Muinuddin Chishti is indeed an ornament to the city of Ajmer. It is one of the holiest places of worship in India not only for the Muslims but also for the people of other faiths who hold the saint the high esteem and reverence. The Khwaja Saheb, as a 'living spirit' of peace and harmony, enjoys universal respect and devotion ever since he set his holy feet on the soil of Hindustan. He has unquestionably been one of the greatest spiritual redeemers of human sufferings. To the faithful and afflicted souls invoking his blessing, he has ever been a never-failing source of moral strength and spiritual enlightenment. Apart from the common people, even the mighty kings of India, both Hindu and Muslim, have paid submissive homage to the great saint and have sought his miraculous aid to solve their problems. The precious buildings and various rich endowments dedicated to the Dargah of Khwaja Saheb are living memorials to and reminders of his continued patronage enjoyed by the people of India throughout the past 750 years.

Hazrat Khwaja Muinuddin Chishti says "He indeed is a true devotee blessed with the love of God, who is gifted with the following three attributes: river-like charity, i.e his sense of charity has no limits and is equally beneficial to all the creatures of God who approach him, Sun-like affection, i.e. his affection may be extended indiscriminately to all like sunlight and Earth-like hospitality, i.e. His loving embrace may be open to all like that of the earth."

We caught the return train, both of us quiet and absorbing the experience. If I had thought the blessings ended there I was mistaken. Next morning I had to take a flight to Kuwait and since there was no connection I would have had to stay the night in Kuwait which I had not planned and was a bit apprehensive. The Kuwait airways flight was delayed and I was able to take a direct British Airways flight from Delhi to London with 3 seats to myself. This after everyone said that were no seats available. My flight landed at

Terminal 1 and I was standing there with 2 heavy suitcases and a roll on, wondering how I will lug these to Terminal 3 where I had to go by train. A young boy wearing a diamond Allah pendant the size of a boiled egg, came by and said "don't worry—I'll take you". He carried all my luggage and escorted me to Terminal 3 and then took off whistling.

I am safely home with my family and pray that everyone gets an opportunity to take these journeys.

Searching for The Divine

> *Soul receives from soul that knowledge, therefore not by book nor from tongue. If knowledge of mysteries come after emptiness of mind, that is illumination of heart.*
>
> *Rumi*

UNESCO has designated 2007 as the 'Year of Rumi" to celebrate the 800th anniversary of Mevlana Jalaluddin Rumi. Rumi was a poet, philosopher and mystic who is being globally commemorated as one of the worlds greatest spiritual and literary figures. Rumi's works have been translated into almost 70 languages and he is touted as being the most read poet in world today.

Rumi was essentially a teacher who traveled with a message about awakening the heart to recognize the divine in a way that people find relevant today. He was also the founder of the Mevlevi order (known for the "Whirling Dervishes").

A disciple of Rumi and a teacher in the Mevlevi tradition, Kabir Helminski explains Rumi's popularity. "Essentially he is a 13th Century poet who has stolen people's hearts today. Much of humanity is in search of a concept of the divine that makes sense—a spirituality that is adequate to our times and Rumi fills that vacuum". Helminski follows in his spiritual Master's footsteps (known as the Mevlevi path) and was in Toronto recently, on a two-day retreat to share authentic knowledge about Rumi and Sufism.

Helminski who lives in Santa Cruz California, found his muse when he was a young student of religion in New York where he went to University. Born a Catholic, he was keenly interested in Eastern traditions and studied Sufism in 1975. At this time he met Camille, also a student of comparative religion with an interest in

Sufism. They got married and started their spiritual journey together traveling frequently Turkey (where Rumi lived and is buried).

In 1980 Helminski was initiated into the Mevlevi tradition. "We travel to Turkey every year to enhance our knowledge and spirituality" says Helminski "because there's a great body of knowledge associated with Islam and Sufism that exists in the works of Rumi". He has also traveled to Iran, Indonesia and India offering a contemporary concept of Sufism—one that both East and West can fit into the modern world. For his dedication to Rumi's scholarship Helminski was initiated as a Shaikh in the Mevlevi order in 1990—an honour few Westerners have achieved.

There are many definitions of Sufism today, but Helminski describes it from Rumi's perspective. "Sufism is a methodology for purifying the heart to make it receptive. Sufis created institutions of higher learning for education about the attributes of the heart like compassion, forgiveness, generosity and love." He goes on to clarify "All Sufism is rooted in Islam. The Quran is the DNA of Rumi's work". In a quatrain, Rumi writes:

I am the servant of the Quran as long as I have life. I am the dust on the path of Mohammad, the Chosen One. If anyone quotes anything except this from my sayings, I am quit of him and outraged by these words.

Nowadays Sufism has many non-serious followers (some referred to as Goofy Sufis). Pointing to this modern day pop phenomenon which he calls "neo-sufism", Helminiski points out that the Mevlevi path he follows is a traditional path. He also points out that it's an ongoing challenge "The Mevlevi path is welcoming to all people but non Muslims are wary that it might lead them to Islam while Muslims are wary that it might lead them out of Islam! Truth is that it will lead them both to a very wide and deep reality that is the heart of Islam".

Camille who is Helminskis wife and partner in spirituality adds "this softer, gentler image of Islam is one without labels". Camille says "Sufism is the mystical heart of Islam and offers the knowledge of purifying the heart using love as a vehicle to God".

Camille's is one of the first women to translate select verses of the Quran into English in her book The Light of Dawn (Shambhala Publications). She is also renowned for her book "Women in Sufism" (Shambhala) which was a labor of love. "In my own journey as a woman on the Sufi path when I looked for sisterhood, there wasn't much out there. Over 18 years of following threads in the history of Sufism I discovered treasures like pearls—the stories of Sufi women and I capture them in my book."

In 1980 the Helminskis started their own publishing company which was formally established in 1988 as The Threshold Society. "Through the Threshold society we carry on spiritual education in many parts of the world keeping Rumi's traditions in the fore front. We try to make this as non-commercial as possible'" They are publishers and editors in another company called The Book Foundation which is a charitable organization based in the United Kingdom. "Through the Book Foundation we promote contemporary commentaries of the Quran. We are involved in an education project to create a series of books and educational resources for Muslims and non-Muslims to present Quranic insights into contemporary issues like ecology, the environment and nature."

As they travel & teach, lecture & learn, play Sufi songs on the Saaz (a Turkish folk instrument), recite names of God in zikr (chanting) and whirl in total submission to the divine, the Helminskis say they are on a continuous journey that offers both inspiration and challenges.

Kabir describes some of the challenges. "It's painful to be a Muslim in America where there is a unique culture of ignoring the human experience. The spirit and humanity are separated. In Sufism both are intermixed as spirit and clay, known and unknown, good and bad. We entered Sufism with innocence never expecting Islam to be at the centre of world conflict." He says wryly and continues "But Sufism, especially the teachings of Rumi provide the remedy for much religious pathology like vitamins for the soul."

In answer to the question about why Sufism and Rumi's philosophy is not mainstream in the Muslim world today he replies "In modern times it's been weakened by scientific application and the influences of Wahabism and extremism."

The Helminski's clarify that Rumi is "not just poetry and whirling as some people view it. Sufism offers wisdom and knowledge; education and a spiritual perception that used properly can develop powerful leaders.

Bearing Witness to Truth and Reconciliation

> *Three things cannot be long hidden: the sun, the moon, and the truth.*
>
> ***Buddha***

When I received the invitation from the Governor General Her Excellency The Right Honourable Michaelle Jean to attend a ceremony at Rideau Hall in Ottawa to listen and learn from the legacy of the Indian Residential Schools, I never thought this would be another poignant journey of the heart. Being an avid fan and admirer of GC, I went because of her.

When I arrived at One Sussex Drive, I was offered a stone or a piece of wood as a token. I was surprised to note that there were only about 100 people there, all seated in semi circles as is the tradition. There were survivors of the residential schools, their children, commissioners, people of faith and some invited guests all seated in a room with a huge mural across one wall painted by an Ojibway artist.

As luck has it, I was sitting next to the door from where Her Excellency The Right Honourable Michaelle Jean made her entrance and I was blown away when in making eye contact with me, she touched her hand to her heart in greeting. I knew then that I was not here due to any co-incidence but that this was another journey of the heart.

That it was. From start to finish it was heart to heart. An elder of the Algonquin Nation opened with a prayer that touched my soul, holding sweet grass for honesty with calls to the Creator to open our ears so we can hear and our hearts so we can feel with compassion. As an introduction we were told about the power of racism and prejudice that overpowered the cries of children taken away from their homes. We were made aware that individuals and nations can only start a new beginning when an apology from the heart leads to the healing of hearts.

Then Michaelle Jean spoke and everyone was in awe. She presented her message in soft words; full of compassion and respect for the communities she was addressing that represented First Nations peoples from all over Canada. I understood why they're called First Nations because they were the original inhabitants of this land thousands of years before the white man came. Her Excellency said that these are the civilizations that shaped our history, not in conflict but in harmony with the circle of life and in harmony with nature.

This description of the First Nations communities feeds into my fascination with this community which began many years ago when I met Ward Churchill and realized that we know very little about the people who lived in these lands long before us. Recently I visited Whistler BC, home of the Squamish and Lil'wat nations and learnt their history so I am hooked.

Her Excellency went on to say that Canada's history is both glorious and dark. The chapter of the residential schools is a dark one. She explained how First Nations parents and grandparents were told that they had nothing to offer their children, so the children were forcefully place in residential schools and stripped of their language, culture and traditions. "We need to consider that all Canadians have lost" she said as tears ran down the faces of almost everyone in the room, "an opportunity to have learnt from the elders of the nation." She said the time has come to travel the road of truth, to speak up and work together. Her next words struck a chord in my heart. "When the present doesn't recognize the mistakes of the past, the future goes wrong."

She stressed that in order to have reconciliation; there must be recognition that something went wrong. The next speaker was Murray Sinclair, a survivor and Chair of the Truth and Reconciliation Commission. He explained that this commission was created because a few courageous survivors decided to speak out, despite their pain and trauma. He mentioned that the residential school movement had affected more than 80,000 Inuit, Metei and others—their spirits were stolen, their families taken away, their culture and traditions destroyed. Mr. Sinclair explained that there will be a series of national events over the next few years where truth will be told.

I heard what it means to "Bear Witness". This is a very important spiritual tradition for First Nations. "To know the truth, we must start telling it. The listeners validate the truth." A group of survivors along with Christian Priests stood up and spoke about the dark past with hope that the time has come to speak out, work together and travel the path of truth and reconciliation. Marie Wilson, the spouse of a survivor said that this chapter of Canada's history belongs to everyone, that this is not about individuals but communal, as the events of the residential schools had far reaching implications.

Then we faced the heartrending portion of seeing and hearing stories of the survivors, many of them grandparents who brought their children and grandchildren with them. They spoke of the pain and humiliation, but with dignity and no hate. Following this, both aboriginal and non-aboriginal youth brought gifts of healing—for friendship, trust, hope, compassion, community for the past and future and we were invited to add our tokens to the baskets as well. I found the rituals very meaningful. Nothing was overdone or dramatized and I wept at their stories, moved and touched by their dignity and humbleness.

I came away with a pin of the logo of truth and reconciliation. A flame to illuminate, transform and purify. I came away with a deep respect for these communities who have so much to teach us and about whom we know so little. I came away with a resolve to be a witness and tell their stories to the world with the same wisdom and respect that they do. I came away with hope for the rest of the world that they too will learn that reconciliation and peace come with an honest recognition that some wrong has been done.

From Su-Shi to Su-Fi: A Unique Eid Celebration

> *The heart's abode it purifies*
> *The dervish into phoenix it transforms*
> *To the Realm of the Divine it leads*
> *'Tis the Remembrance of the Lord,*
>   *Pir Nureddin al-Jerrahi*

The su-shi part of my family i.e. my offspring of the sunni-shia variety plus my grandson the Mexi-Paki did some interesting explorations this Eid. We were all inspired by Sheikh Tevfik Adoner of the Jerrahi Sufi order of Canada, who had come to our home on 15 Ramzan for zikr. Tevfik Baba is an incredible human being whose business card reads "faqir"(servant). When I invited him, he was fasting and hosting people that evening but he left the gathering to cook a meal for dozens of people (which was his job that night) and came all the way to be part of our family zikr for one hour. In this short time he managed to renew, refresh and uplift our souls in ways that will remain forever embedded in the hearts of some guests, consisting of Christians, Hindus, Buddhists and Jews. It was a wholly organic experience, from the heart to the heart!

So on Eid day when we discovered that some masjids were still debating whether itsEid or not, we decided to try The New Canadian Sufi Cultural Centre, the Dergah of the Jerrahi Sufis. It was a unique experience from the start. All families were in the same section upstairs where there are Turkish carpets and long cushions. Women are to one side on a raised platform and men a bit lower (quite the change from the norm!). Kids run around freely. It was delightful for once to experience Eidprayers with my whole family. The namaz was led by Tevfik Baba with a short khutba (sermon) in English, followed by everyone walking in a circle, wishing Eid Mubarak.

Following this ritual we were invited for Turkish breakfast in the basement. Interestingly there was a bazaar set up alongside, with community members selling pure honey, shoes, jewelry etc. at giveaway prices. It was very revealing to note that the market went hand in hand with the worship, neither taking away from the other. A reminder that we are living a world where we have to work, play, interact and incorporate our spirituality into the reality of this life. Next to Tevfik Baba sat a Church Minister invited from the neighborhood church, keen on making contacts and building bridges. These bridges I noted were being built one step at a time through love, warmth, hospitality, sharing of food, stories and music. Our Eid was complete and unique. The sons and grandson loved the freedom of moving around and sitting to eat with family. We absorbed the ambience and will come back for more—the soul remains hungry for more nurturing. The Jerrahis do this with knowledge, grace and compassion.

The Colors of Autumn Merge: with the Color of Islam

> *On the day you see the light of your own true Self, you'll rejoice!*
> *But if you only see forms which from the beginning were in you,*
> *and don't die to them or know them,*
> *how can you stand the light?*
>
> *From the Gospel of Thomas*

Fonthill United church is nestled on a hill in a small town called Fonthill, near Niagara Falls. It's a long drive from Toronto, but how many people would be out on the road on a Sunday morning at 8 am? Just a couple of "eternal optimists" and flocks of birds enjoying the end of summer. So we found ourselves in for an easy drive.

With the beginning of vibrant colours of autumn on the trees overlooking the church, there was a sign outside saying THE COLOURS OF ISLAM. Perhaps it was this unusual sign that attracted a large number of people to come out to church this Sunday in September—a leap of faith for the visionary Minister, Rev. Dr. Garry van Bruchem who had invited two Muslims to offer a Muslim service in a Christian church.

As the congregation settled, there was a call to worship from the pulpit of the church. This was no ordinary call. It was the azaan (Muslim call to prayer) recited with feeling and passion by a young man who has an extremely melodious and soulful voice. The vibration of the azaan could be felt up to the stained glass ceiling and I saw two women in the front row, wipe their eyes. After the call to prayer, there was pin drop silence as the congregation absorbed what had just happened. Perhaps one of many firsts in this part of the country where a Muslim call to prayer in a church, is not the norm. When I translated the azaan for the congregation, they were moved.

The entire service was a combination of readings from the Qur'an and the Bible, and sayings of Jesus and Mohammad. We played Sufi soul music and the congregation who had thought that there is no music in Islam were thrilled to the core. We spoke about the united colours of Islam i.e diversity within Islam as well Islam's relationship with other faith traditions. We expounded on the similarities between the two faiths and it was a message received with open hearts and minds. People came and hugged us and said they were so grateful for the message. There were also tough questions at the end, but when we begin with a call to worship, followed by a hymn from the United church hymn book, the path is already easy. We were refreshed, rejuvenated, revived and rejoiced at the opportunity to reiterate that while there are differences, it's our commonalities as humans and as people of faith and spirit that bind us together.

Ever so often, in the far reaches of a small town, we re-discover that humanity is really one community.

Officiating a Marriage is Alright and a Woman's Right

> *What women rightly long for is spiritual and moral initiative from a man, not spiritual and moral domination.*
>
> **John Piper**

A story in the news and doing rounds on the Internet is about a Muslim wedding in Lucknow, India last month, which was officiated by a woman and had female witnesses. "Women-led Muslim wedding sparks debate in India"

This unorthodox move is totally outside the norm, because Muslim marriages are traditionally officiated by a man, and also witnessed by males. Interestingly, the All India Muslim Personal law Board approved the ceremony led by a woman, much to the angst of Islamic seminaries. Women rights activists see this as a "symbolic step forward for Muslim women" but the story has sparked a fiery controversy being denounced by conservative Islamic institutions as an affront to Islam. There are also personal comments posted on websites carrying the story. One comment reads "this sounds like an appropriate time to start a violent jihad."

Well, I hate to inform the detractors and Jihadists that in order to grab all women activists, they'll have to travel to North America. While I'm thoroughly impressed at this breakthrough in India, my sisters in the struggle need to know that there are others who are also working for dignity and equality for Muslim women as mandated by Islam and practiced by Prophet Mohammad. Sometimes a major step has to be taken outside the box, to break the status quo and smash the barriers of patriarchy.

Recently, I had the honour and privilege of performing my first Muslim marriage in Toronto. The challenge wasn't just officiating over the marriage but presiding over an interfaith union. The boy is Muslim and the girl, a Jewish feminist who wanted women in the forefront. They approached me because they had heard about my leading prayer and thought I might want to add another "bullet point" to my bio!

I asked my religious mentor whether this is valid in Islam. He said "of course" explaining that the Muslim Marriage ceremony (called Nikah) is actually a pre-Islamic tradition taken from the Jews by the pagans and later adapted by the Muslims. He also explained that as long as the conditions of the contract are met, any respected member of the community could perform the Nikah.

As a passionate interfaith advocate and someone who has prayed respectfully in churches, synagogues, mosques and temples, I wanted this marriage to have an integrated spirit. After all, I explained to the families, when the Quran refers to Jews as "people of the book", we have more in common than differences. So why not make this a bridge-building exercise and learn from each other? To give them credit, the young couple trusted me implicitly and the families agreed.

It didn't take me long to learn that Jewish and Muslim marriages have some similarities. The ketubeh, the mahr or marriage gift and the presence of witnesses are some commonalities. The wedding was very well organized and attended by about 250 people; mostly families of the bride and groom but also guests of diverse cultures and faiths. Everything from the décor (a Chuppah on stage) to the dress (the bride wore a traditional red Pakistani outfit) and the music (an eclectic ensemble of East and West) was reflective of both traditions.

On stage was the bride's uncle, the woman who would perform the legal service, the female ring bearer and I. The bride's uncle explained the significance of the Chuppah as well as smashing a glass by the groom.

When it came time for me to perform the Nikah, I have to admit I was nervous. I started by reciting opening of the Quran,

(Fatiha) and once I translated it, I felt totally humbled and uplifted. I knew I was doing this for God and He was witness to my intention. I explained the procedure including that in Islam the woman gives the offer of marriage (the shocked looks on faces showed many people were unaware of this). Then I quoted from the chapter 49 of the Quran where we read ".. We created you from a single (pair) of a male and a female, and made you into nations and tribes, that you may know each other". What better way to know one another, I said, than the union of two people, two faiths and two cultures? Instead of a long-drawn sermon, I read from Rumi and the Nikah was completed by going through all the steps and ending in the final contract, which is part of both Jewish and Muslim traditions. It was a profound and moving experience.

Once the ceremony was over, there were the usual tears and congratulations. The family of the bride and groom hugged me and said they were very inspired by the ceremony, while sceptics patted me on the back. But my efforts were fully validated when some young people, thrilled at the revolutionary idea of a woman presiding over a marriage, invited me to New York and Los Angeles to perform weddings—both Jewish and Muslim!

Helena's Voyage and Paul's Journey

> Love expects no reward. Love knows no fear.
> Love Divine gives—does not demand.
> Love thinks no evil; imputes no motive.
> To Love is to share and serve.
>
> *Sivananda*

While I've always believed that nothing in life is a co-incidence, there are times when this feeling is so clearly reinforced that it's like an awakening. Something like this happened to me a few weeks ago.

Last year I spoke on a panel at an event held by University of Toronto called ABRAHAM'S LIGHT. As with public events, I met many people and one of them was a man who said he would have a book out in 2008. I filed that information at the back of my head. Few weeks ago I got an email from Paul Harbridge reminding me where we had met and asking if I would review his book Helena's Voyage. At this point neither Paul nor the book meant anything to me other than an author promoting a book. I had just had a new grandchild and was a bit selfishly involved in my own life and worries about how to make a living. So I said we could meet later in the month when I had more time, but Paul called back and said he would drop off a copy.

On Sunday the doorbell rang and I was a bit irritated because I wasn't expecting anyone and had my grandson in my arms. I opened the door and in an instant something flashed through the eyes of the man standing there and hit my heart. There was immense pain in Paul Harbridge's eyes as he stood there holding his book. Later he told me that the sight of a baby in my arms made him weep on the way home. Only later I discovered that Paul's 18 year old daughter Helena had died in her sleep and this book is dedicated to her. Although this is Paul and Helena's story there is a deep personal connection. I realized when I saw Paul standing at my doorstep that my life was meant to be a bridge for others—the only tears I could weep would have to be for others and that my purpose in life was not me—but people like Paul crying out for spiritual aid! How foolish and petty are my worries compared to the enormous weight carried by people like Paul. I was humbled beyond belief and thrown into action.

I met Paul the following week to get details and this is his journey about Helena's voyage. Paul Harbridge is a speech language pathologist living in Toronto. He had two children, a son named Daniel who is 25 and a daughter named Helena. Paul's wife is from Spain so he says that he always felt his kids carried in them a dual heritage—their Spanish heritage which Paul associates with the grandeur of Spain when three traditions thrived there. Paul and his family often travelled to Spain.

Paul was raised as an evangelical Christian but later he became a devout Catholic. He says he was religious but never spiritual until Helena passed away. Helena was his love and joy.

"Helena had a special sparkle, she was full of life". When Helena was a child she had asthma and would call herself " a sick girl". However she grew up to be strong and played in golf tournaments becoming a top golfer for the Canadian Junior Golf Association in 2004. Academically Helena was so bright that she got a scholarship to University of West Georgia and went to study there. Helena was always helpful with other kids and was known to have a warm and loving heart.

On Easter Saturday in 2006, Helena was getting ready to come home to her family in Toronto. She called in the morning and said she was going to take a nap and call later in the evening to give her flight details. She never woke up. The University found her the next day when she didn't call home and the parents panicked. Doctors said it was some form of heart arrhythmia.

The family flew to Georgia and brought Helena's body home. That night Helena's brother Daniel stood in the porch of their home and cried so much that a mound of tears was frozen near the door. Paul says he remembers that night—he felt his heart would burst. He looked up to heaven and asked God "How am I going to get through this? What am I going to do with all the love I have for my daughter?" He says he heard a response as though from Helena. The response was "Find a spiritual path and spread the love. Look after people and give them love."

Paul and his wife started reading, mediation and contemplation. It wasn't easy. "Pictures of Helena would flash in front of my eyes and if there had been a way to leave life to go and be with her, I would have done so". At this point in life Paul heard Karen Armstrong on TV and she mentioned two books. One was The History of God and the other was The Ornament of the World: How Muslims, Jews, and Christians Created a Culture of Tolerance in Medieval Spain by Maria Rosa Menocal. Paul got both books and started to read them. He says "I was fascinated by the connectedness between the three Abrahamic traditions".

Partway through the books, he and his wife went to Spain to see his in-laws and he read the rest of the books there. "Reading about Spain in Spain was more inspirational than I could have thought. Here is where an idea took seed in my mind to write a story about a Jewish girl whose grandfather was a physician in the court of Spain." Paul is not an artist or a painter but he doodles. "One day I doodled a picture of a teddy bear in a boat entering a Jewish City—the teddy bear became a young girl and it took me exactly half a day to write Helena's Voyage." What about the illustrations? "My wife encouraged me to try and draw but that was hard. I drew the last page first—it took me 12 hours for every illustration. But I did it and that was how Helena's Voyage came about." Paul's son Daniel put the book on You Tube and made the DVD adding spiritual music.

For Paul this was also his spiritual awakening. "Every time I went to the computer to write, I used to light two candles. One for Helena and one for her Spanish grandfather".

Paul says his other purpose for writing the book is "at the time I was reading Armstrong and Menocal I was also seeing images on TV of parents holding their dead children, killed by bombs, in the Middle East and because I had lost Helena, I knew their grief for the first time in my life. That too influenced my decision to write Helena's Voyage."

I asked Paul what is his vision for Helena's Voyage and he said "I think my real dream is to one day seeing Jews, Christians and Muslims united (not one religion but united in purpose) to bring the word of God to a broken secular materialistic numbers-focused world. To tell others that there is a God that loves us all, that there are universal divine laws to guide us, that there is a Spirit to strengthen us and give us wisdom, that true happiness comes when we submit ourselves to doing God's will, and that love is the only true force in this universe for God is love. Wouldn't it be wonderful to see us, our differences set aside, our commonality assumed, all working side by side to do God's work? That is my dream."

In some ways Paul Harbridge and Helena's Voyage have reinforced that need for spreading God's love and God's word. I want to help get the word out because there are many different ways this is being done and I want to be a miniscule part of that labor of love.

Spirit of the East: A Sacred Music Concert

Mahatma Gandhi said Always aim at complete harmony of thought and word and deed. Always aim at purifying your thoughts and everything will be well.

Perhaps it was the purity of intention and sincerity of thought behind the event that made this evening a mystical, magical, musical experience for everyone who came and for those who participated. The idea for this event came to me when I was rehearsing with a group of artists from different Eastern traditions, and found that there was a synergy in the sur and taal (rhythm) that needed to be tapped. Hence SPIRIT OF THE EAST was born.

South Asians are the largest ethnic minority in Canada so, while we may compete over cricket and gossip about politics, the one thing that binds us together is our common heritage and love of music—which knows no boundaries. Hinduism, Sikhism and Islam are the fastest growing faiths in Canada but the least known. To have the 3 traditions on one stage was not only extraordinary but genuinely reflective of this multi-faith, multi-cultural, multicolored mosaic that many of us call home.

The audience consisted of Hindus, Muslims, Christians, Jews, Sikhs, Buddhists and Zoroastrians. We started our program with whirling because this is a symbolic ritual based on the universal idea that everything revolves around something that is bigger than itself physically as well as spiritually. Rumi says "Have you seen a spinning top get up and whirl by itself? Surely whoever whirls has Someone spinning him."

Our young samazen David Coskun, learnt to 'turn' shortly after he learned to walk. A student at University of Waterloo where he is studying to become a mechanical engineer, David had the audience in a trance inviting them with his movements into the circle of love and light. He set the stage for what was to follow.

A painter paints pictures on canvas. But musicians paint their pictures on silence.

ArticulateAzalea Ray and her accompanying artists: Kiran Morarjiwhose fingers dance on Tabla; Hector Cepade playing for the first time with South Asians—brilliant on bass guitar; Dr. Sundar Viswanathan sublime on woodwinds and Bendana Singh soulfully strumming her guitar began with a Bhajan like we've never heard before. The start in English invoking Allah, Shiva, Kali, Jesus, Wahay Guru was stunning. When Azalea chanted Bismillah, I could feel the beginning of goose pimples, because she does not sing, she IS the music. It was an offering that was felt by everyone and the audience was mesmerized. She sang from her heart, the musicians played with their souls and the audience absorbed it all as a spiritual experience. A few said they transcended.

The Sikh scriptures contain hymns or "shabads" which have universal themes of invoking connectedness and oneness with the one God and humanity. Shabad literally means to "cut the ego" as it carries with it the wisdom and strength to do so. It is said in Sikh scriptures that one who has conquered the ego, has won or conquered the world, "Man jeetay jug jeet".

Onkar Singh sang a Shabad in his soulful and deeply resonant voice. Later he sand a Sufi ballad and explained how his young son told him it was just like a kirtan. Accompanied on the tabla by Jasvinder Hunjan who says that music is his religion and his greatest passion. The way Jasvinder's fingers dance on the Tabla is expressive of this passion. Their invocation to the Creator was:

You are the very power behind each breath and thus life. We pray and express our devotion to you to help us (through the day to day of life and it's stresses) as without you, we are merely meek and weak.

Munni and Afzal Subhani came on stage and vowed the audience with three very upbeat pieces including 2 Qawwalis. They sang Laal Meree and the audience joined in clapping their hands. Their last piece Allah Hu had everyone joining in. It was amazing to see Jasvinder accompany them on the Tabla with no difficulty.

The audience was then treated to a new composition written which was performed with heartfelt reverence by Azalea. The words are:

"Ik Tu Hi Sahara, hai Tu Hi Kinara, Saray jag ke aye malik sub kuch hai Tumhara".

You alone are the sustainer, You alone are the shore, Oh Lord of the worlds, everything we have is yours!

The finale was the Qawwali "Chaap Tilak" by Ameer Khusro. Azalea spent some time explaining to the audience where she was coming from. Her entire being was infused with the passion of the poet and the magic of the music. There was some innovation and she started repeating Allah Hu, it was resounding. Fact that the singer and musicians were from varying traditions was not lost on the audience. Here we had a true bridging of the gap—a synergy of sound beyond barriers. The ambience, the passion, the purity brought people to their feet in a standing ovation for the singers and musicians.

In the Uppanishads we read about mystical and philosophical truths.

People call for hymns, without understanding the significance of a hymn. The hymn is THAT from which the favour of the Gods arises, as the Earth, from all whatsoever that exists arises. The great hymn is creation.

Finding Peace in Kincardine

> Load the ship and set out. No one knows for certain whether the vessel will sink or reach the harbor.
> Cautious people say, "I'll do nothing until I can be sure." Merchants know better.
> If you do nothing, you lose. Don't be one of those merchants who won't risk the ocean.
>
> *Rumi*

It seems that once we decide to give our hearts to spirituality, it follows us wherever we go—or we find spirituality in life wherever we go.

The journey continues as we drive through vast lands from Lake Ontario across the plains to the other end, Lake Huron. Blue skies, farmlands, birds singing, cows grazing and very little habitation. I wonder sometimes what I am doing here?

I look for signs and all I see are fields and clouds in the shape of an X. I have been seeing this cross or X continuously for about a year and I ask people what it means as a symbol. Lately someone says it reflects a combination of the Cross in Christianity, the Star of David for Judaism and the Islamic Star in the Crescent—well since I live, breath and dream interfaith dialogue this resonates a bit for me. I'm awaiting more insight. Perhaps there's a secret message I don't see:

The breeze at dawn has secrets to tell you.
Don't go back to sleep.
You must ask for what you really want.
Don't go back to sleep.
People are going back and forth across the doorsill where the two worlds touch.
The door is round and open.
Don't go back to sleep.

We arrive at The Lakefront Bread and Breakfast Inn where a reservation has been made for us. However there is no one there and the place is not locked. The entire office cum house is empty and full of artifacts which could be antique. We walk around observing that the owners must have been connected to shipping as almost everything has a shipping connection. So we find the log cabin on the side of the house, right in front of the beach and the waves and make ourselves at home. Later the owners come home and we meet the amazing Katrena Johnston—a spiritual woman if I ever met one. She does many fundraising efforts for kids in third world countries and has also made skirts from ties—yes men's ties. She shows me one and I'm amazed at her creativity.

She points to a section of the beach outside her cabin which is a healing place. How so? This was all originally native land and this 8 by 6 section is a place where animals come and are attracted. Later I see my first beaver—a fat blob with a flat tail it bobbles and ducks in the water eating fish and then waddles out to the healing spot, stops a bit and goes back in the water. Katrena tells me deer come and pray at this spot as well. I go down later to take in some of the ambience. I look up for a sign and the clouds are in a cross picture. At night we hear the gentle sound of waves and I am healed.

Ready to face the questions next day. I present on Women in Islam and although most of the audience is very receptive, one lady bombards me with hostile questions. I am quite mellow in answering and she tones down. There are hugs and kisses and we find our way home.

For years, copying other people, I tried to know myself.

Journeys to the Center of My Soul

> *When you do things from your soul, you feel a river moving in you, a joy*
>
> *Rumi*

I was invited to SUNY—State University of New York at Brockport to participate in a conference on Edward Said. It was interesting that this conference was entirely for academia but the hosts must have sensed the closet "academic' in me and invited me as the keynote speaker from a non-academic perspective. I was delighted because I've been to Brockport before and had made some connections of the heart including a young Moroccon student who calls me mother.

Brockport is a small US town near Rochester, mostly white middle and upper class. The place I stayed is called The Victorian B & B and is reflective of the true heart of America—not the capitalism and materialism we see around us. Run by two Sisters, the Victorian B & B is quaint, old fashioned and extremely comfortable. Brockport downtown is a 10 minute walk with one of everything i.e. coffee shop, bookstore, cinema, hairdresser etc. River runs besides it and was a joy. I stayed four days and would walk, pick up a sandwich and read—something I haven't done in a while.

Two amazing things happened. First I met a Professor and his wife who are dervishes. Both have lived and worked in Morocco and are the students of an Iraqi teacher from Baghdad. He is American and she is Spanish. First moment I met her I knew we had a spiritual connection that went far back. They both shared deeply spiritual and personal stories of sufi retreats where they were able to give up smoking and are now staunch vegetarians doing zikr and whirling on a regular basis. She is also a psychic healer and realized that my body and soul were quite exhausted from the work I was doing non-stop for the past two weeks so she indulged me in a mixture of reiki,

(Reiki is a Japanese technique for stress reduction and relaxation that also promotes healing. It is administered by "laying on hands" and is based on the idea that an unseen "life force energy" flows through us and is what causes us to be alive. If one's "life force energy" is low, then we are more likely to get sick or feel stress, and if it is high, we are more capable of being happy and healthy.) aromatherapy and prayer. I felt newly revived and refreshed.

I also met a Mormon couple where he is studying Arabic and Islamic history because he feels a connection between Mormon tradition and Islam—very interesting.

I taught one class on Gender and Islam and came home quite inspired by my not-so-coincidental meeting with many wonderful teachers. I am humbled.

Take someone who doesn't keep score,
Who's not looking to be richer,
or afraid of losing,
Who has not the slightest interest even
is his own personality:
He's free.

The Call of Rumi—from Konya

> *Out beyond ideas of wrongdoing and right doing, there is a field. I'll meet you there.*
>
> *When the soul lies down in that grass, the world is too full to talk about.*
>
> *Ideas, language, even the phrase "each other" doesn't make any sense.*
>
> *Rumi*

Since I became interested and fascinated with Rumi, I wanted to visit Konya—the place where he is buried. But I waited because I am told that one gets to visit Rumi when the time is ready and he beckons.

Last year we were on a visit to Jerusalem—our yearly Pilgrimage so to speak. We planned to visit Konya on our way back as our trip was to be via Turkey and Konya is in Turkey.

In Jerusalem I have a Jewish Sufi friend Yaqub Ibn Yusuf who owns and runs a Sufi bookstore and I usually try to meet him. When I visited Yaqub, I excitedly told him about our plans for Konya and he got animated. "Konya" he said "I visit there regularly and have a good friend. Could you give him this CD for me?" Yaqub gave me the contact for his friend Hasan Hussain in Konya and a CD and I said we would try to find him.

We were travelling on standby tickets and when we checked the flight from Istanbul to Konya on our day of departure, we found that the flight had filled up and no seats were available. We were very disappointed but had to connect from Istanbul for Toronto anyway so we arrived at Istanbul airport ready to come home.

Suddenly Sohail said "lets go to the gate for Konya anyway". It was a whim but since we had time, I went along. The gate agent told us the flight was full but for some reason we waited. Soon there was a commotion and we heard the gate agents saying that the luggage of one family who were connecting to this flight, had not arrived and they could not travel. Most of the passengers for Konya had already boarded when the agent saw us sitting there and asked us if we still wanted to do. Of course we ran and got the last two seats to Konya.

We had booked a hotel in Konya online so we had no idea where we were staying. It was Saturday afternoon and when we asked the concierge where everything was located, much to our delight he told us we were walking distance from all of Rumi's heritage building and very close to the tomb of Hazrat Shams Tabrizi, who was Rumi's mentor and teacher. According to Sufi tradition, one must first visit the tomb of the teacher and then the student. So we immediately set off to pay our respects and found the tomb within two minutes of our hotel.

Konya is a like something outwardly. One feels disconnected with the materialism and commercialism of real life and in a special place. We paid our respects to Hazrat Shams Tabrizi and then set off to find where the Rumi whirling takes place because we were told that it only happens on Saturday nights so we didn't want to miss it.

Soon we were lost because every building was a Rumi monument and due to language difficulty we couldn't figure out where to go. Suddenly a tour bus stopped near us and Sohail spoke to one of the people on the bus. They said they were going to the stadium where the Rumi music and whirling takes place and would be happy to take us with them provided we stood all the way as all the seats were taken. We happily hopped on and were taken to the stadium.

Having come un-prepared, we found that all tickets for the program had to be purchased online and there was no ticket booth. But we knew Rumi had called us so far so we would find a way. We made our way through thousands of people and found an officer dealing with the crowds. We told him our sorry story and how far we had come and that we would be happy to pay double for the tickets. He took us to a cordoned off area and told us to wait. We waited for 20 minutes while we saw people going in. Suddenly the officer appeared with two tickets for us and refused to take any money.

We were able to enjoy the Rumi ensemble to the fullest. It's an experience I will never forget. On a round stage in the middle of the stadium, an orchestra plays Sufi music and chants while dozens of white robed Dervishes whirl in ecstasy. We were in ecstasy as well.

We got back to the hotel late night and Sohail discovered he had lost his cell phone in the stadium crowds. Never mind we said. This is meant to be and after all it's only a phone. We made the necessary phone calls to our son in Toronto to cancel stuff and went to bed. Next morning Sohail was chatting with the concierge who asked how the program was and Sohail mentioned his lost phone. The concierge said "you will find it as Mevlana doesn't want anyone to leave Konya unhappy". He then called the stadium who said they had found a few phones. A taxi drive later, the phone was back with us.

Such is the mysticism of Konya and Rumi.

That was not all. That day I remembered to call Hasan Hussain. He said he has a store one block from where we were and invited us to come and meet him. I took the CD and we went to his apartment on top of a carpet shop. Hasan used to be a whirling Dervish but now had retired due to age and with his family, he ran a wellness center. We did not have time to indulge in the wellness rituals but had tea with him. He said he makes his own wellness organic creams. As we got up to leave he looked at me and said "you have a problem with your knees. Let me give you something". I was shocked because I had said nothing to him but had been dealing with arthritis in my knees and lot of pain. He gave me four cases of cream—one small one for travel and explained how to use it with full confidence that it will cure my ailment. Such faith. In the same faith I brought the cream back with me and used it for a month. Since then I have never had a pain in my knees and my arthritis is completely cured. I have referred many people to Hasan Hussain and some have gone and spent a week at this wellness clinic with great results.

Konya was mystical, spiritual, magical and I wait for the day we will be called back by Rumi.

Operation One Heart at a Time

To me, spirituality is about two things: The liberation of consciousness from all illusion, so that the true nature can shine and an embodiment in life that is an alternative to the patterns of manipulation and greed that dominate our current culture. John Bund

I was invited to British Columbia for a National Women's Retreat. Since I was going to be in the area anyway, I contacted some of the churches to see if they would like me to speak there, and the response was heartwarming. Before I knew it, I was booked to speak at three locations in Vancouver and one in Victoria. My entire trip was an experience to share.

My first invitation was from Mt. Seymour United Church in North Vancouver which is close to where I was staying with my dear friends, the Belsitos. It was a coincidence that this is the church that they attend. We discovered that the flyer for this church was positioned as "Bridging the Gulf between East and West"—me-thinks that some people thought this was about Eastern and Western Canada and since that is impossible, they didn't come! Once we set the record straight however, it was exciting and the dialogue was at a high level.

Jen-Beth from Mt. Seymour has lived in many parts of the world including Indonesia, so she had some idea of where I was coming from. I had taken a CD of Sufi music and they were thrilled to play it in their sanctuary. Somehow Sufi music resounds well in a place of worship. About 70 people turned up and asked some leading questions from sharia to Sufism. The response and interaction was amazing.

Later that day I was interviewed on a BC TV channel called Studio 4. This interview done by Fanny Kiefer was one of the best interviews I have had to date. Apart from the fact that BC premier Gordon Campbell was on the same show, Fanny asked me something no one has. She asked "with all the misinformation and controversy out there, would you like to divorce the term Jihad from your life or reclaim it?" What a brilliant question! I told her "reclaim it for sure" and while I was saying that, I realized that is what I have set out to do. It also made me think "do we want to take the word "colonization" out of the English language because of its impact on a large part of the world? Or the word "occupied" because occupation had caused so much death and destruction?" No of course not—what we (I) want to do is ensure that the true meaning of these words is understood and practiced so that the negative connotations can be removed by our own actions and replaced by a noble and humane understanding. I want to clarify that while 'armed Jihad' is no longer valid in the 21st. century, spiritual Jihad (jihad here meaning struggle) is needed.

On Sunday morning I was invited by the Canadian Memorial United Church, downtown. This also has a Center for Peace. Not only is this Church a thing of beauty, the turnout was surprising—about 300 people came. I was touched and humbled by the fact that the church choir had found the words and practiced Sufi chants for the service. Imagine. In this peaceful and beautiful sanctuary, the choir sang Subhan Allah(God is Great) followed by a zikr of Bismillahir Rahmanar Rahim and the entire congregation joined in. It was spell binding and some people had their eyes closed with tears down their faces. Let me tell you that a church choir is powerful and with their organ, the sound of Allah Allah Subhanallah reached the skies. I could only say Subhan Allah again and again and my heart gave thanks and blessings for the music director who took pains to find the words, their translation and put it to music. Of course credit goes to the visionary Minister Bruce Sanguin who made this possible. This is the FIRST time I have heard such heartfelt and genuine zikr in the church. Allah be Praised. Later I spoke to the kids and showed them my Janamaz (prayer rug) and tasbih (prayer beads) and they responded with the true curiosity of kids. One parent came to me later and said "when I saw how the kids responded to you, I knew you were the right person for this work as kids are instinctively honest". What a compliment. Feedback was warm—I am invited back.

Next day I spoke at the School of Theology and chapel at UBC—another thing of beauty with high rafters and huge French windows on one side. The Minister there is a young lady and she welcomed me warmly. I was so touched at her sensitivity when she gently asked me that if I felt offended standing in the front where there is a cross on the wall behind me, she could turn the crowd around so that I face the other way and I thought to myself, do we have this same compassion and respect for others? The turnout was impressive because the talk was titled "Jihad for Dummies" and some people came only because they were tickled by the title. Later there were many questions. UBC has to be one of the most tranquil and esthetically beautiful campus I have seen—perhaps I haven't seen them all.

Next day I invited to take a tour of the Ismaili Jamaat Khana known as Darkhana which is one of six throughout the world and was inaugurated by The Aga Khan for his 25th anniversary. The monument is a study in modern and traditional architecture. Designed by Italian Bruno Freschi, the Jamaat Khaana reflects spirituality and light from the word go. The courtyard with a fountain is out of Spain; the entire façade is covered with calligraphy and the theme is that of an Octagon which resonates throughout the building. It was a great privilege that I was given a guided tour by a young man well versed in the history of the monument and taken to their prayer hall. Talk about stereo-types. I have heard people (who have never been inside a Jamaat Khaana) say that Ismailis pray in front of the photo of the Aga Khan. Well, what do you know? They don't! The prayer space is so spiritual and sublime, that I wanted to kneel there. There is a small divider between women and men's side, a place for the Imam, lots of seating on the sides for their elders and carpets with the Octagon embedded in them in sync with a sun roof shining light right through. The entire building is a serene place of meditation and reflection. Downstairs they have classrooms and an impressive library plus offices.

On Friday morning I took the ferry to Victoria Island. Now if there is a place that is like Heaven on earth, it's Victoria in cherry blossom season. Unbelievably stunning. Of course I took a camera but forgot to take pictures I was so spellbound.

In Victoria I attended a women's retreat where the speaker was Daphne Bramham, author of a new book called "The Secret Lives of Saints—Child Brides and Lost Boys in Canada's polygamous Mormon Sect". I was riveted because she started her talk by saying that while Canadian soldiers are fighting the Taliban in Afghanistan for women's freedoms and rights, right here in Canada there exists a fundamentalist Mormon sect in Bountiful B.C., where young brides and polygamy play out with nearly forced child labour and extortion. When Daphne heard I was there, she said we must talk and I bought her book in which she inscribed "we have to work together on many of these issues". These issues transcend cultural and religious barriers to reinforce that women have to work hard to change the lives of our young girls. This book is a MUST READ for all of us who think we are liberated by being in North America and that the struggle for freedom exists all over the world.

On my last day in Victoria, I gave two talks and a First Metropolitan United Church. Almost 300 people came out and were full of curiosity and questions. Here too, the music director led the choir in sufi zikr. In the workshop someone asked me, "are there any Mosques where Christian women are invited to preach and perhaps the Muslim congregation could hear the words of our hymns* [see example below] which are very beautiful and uplifting in praise of God?" My answer—I don't know.

This trip has opened many doors and has brought much self-reflection. I feel blessed to have met so many wonderful people but my heart and soul say thanks to my friends Larry and Tania Belsito who drove me everywhere in Vancouver and put their life on hold for me. When I said thanks, Tania said "you are my sister" and I believe that I am her soul sister.

A verse from a hymn:

*Deep in our hearts, there is a common vision
Deep in our hearts there is a common song
Deep in our hearts there is a common story
Telling creation that we are one*

*Deep in our hearts, there is a common purpose
Deep in our hearts there is a common goal
Deep in our hearts there is a sacred message
Justice and peace in harmony*

AFTERWORD
by Ya'qub ibn Yusuf

When I first visited Jerusalem as a speaker for the conference "Facing Tomorrow," we were allocated a student who would accompany us as a kind of ambassador. My student was a young man named Assaf Amgar, and as we chatted I found that he was a musician and a very spiritual person. When he discovered that I love Sufism, he took me to the Olam Qatan bookstore, where I met the proprietor, Ya'qub ibn Yusuf. I was fascinated to discover a bookstore in Jerusalem which sells Sufi books and music CDs, along with Jewish, Far Eastern, New Age, etc.). I was fascinated by Ya'qub himself, who calls himself a Jewish Sufi. Together with Assaf and Ya'qub, I visited the home of Ihab and Ora Balha in Jaffa. Ihab is a Muslim Sufi who leads a group of mostly secular Israelis in Zikr, while his Jewish wife, Ora, teaches them the dance of the whirling dervishes. Since then Ya'qub and I have become warm friends, and I saw on the internet these stories that he wrote. People ask me, "How can you be a Jewish Sufi?" Well, the answer is in these stories, which I am honoured to share. It seems that nothing in life is a coincidence.

Raheel

Two Stories of Sufi Initiation

Both these stories, about how I became Ya'qub and about my experience on the Temple Mount, are pieces of my spiritual autobiography... which I have yet to write. The first is a story that I tell—day in, day out—when I meet people at my spiritual bookstore in Jerusalem, Olam Qatan. Well, I usually tell a shorter version of this story. Speaking of names, the name for the store comes from Rabbi Yitzhaq of Acre, a 14th Century Kabbalist who, it turns out, was familiar with Sufis. He said, "Every human being is a micro-cosm (olam qatan) and the world as a whole is a macro-human being (adam gadol)." The Hebrew expression "olam qatan" is commonly used when people want to say, "It's a small world."

The first story is my answer to the question, why does this Israeli Jew from America have an Arabic name? The second is a story I hardly ever tell. I think it happened that same summer, and it goes much deeper. I wrote up these two stories and shared them in my Facebook group, "Judaism & Sufism," and now I'm happy to let

Raheel include them in her book. How indeed does a Jewish fellow from Brooklyn go from being Joshua Drexler Heckelman ("Drexler" so that I'd carry my mother's family name) to Yaqub ibn Yusuf?

It was in the Spring of 1976, when I was 24, that I first "took hand" with Sidi Sheikh Muhammad and became his disciple. I had come to Israel after a couple of years of intensive study with Rabbi Zalman Schachter, both at the University of Manitoba in Winnipeg, Canada, where he taught "The Psychology of Religion," and more intimately in his home, with a small circle of friends. Of all the teachings he laid out before us, it was the Hasidic teachings of Rebbe Nahman of Bratzlav that most spoke to my heart. It was there that I found a universal spiritual vision which was clearly expressed in Jewish terms. In his "Torah of the Void" Reb Nahman showshow the whole of creation is surrounded by the Infinite Light of God, and yet he accounts for scientific materialism and existential despair in his world-view. This meant a lot to me, as someone who spent his teen-age years immersed in the writings of Franz Kafka and the music of Bob Dylan. I found that the key to Rebbe Nahman's teachings was in what Reb Zalman described as "the archetype of the Tzaddiq"—the figure of the spiritual master which is embodied by certain people, but which also exists as a potential within oneself. I saw that Hasidism is similar to other spiritual traditions in this regard!

I got a great overview of spiritual possibilities with Reb Zalman, and I was looking for ways of going deeper. Buddhist meditation took me deeper, but in a way that was focused to bodily awareness, and made no use of my stronger faculties of heart and mind. In the Fall of 1975 I completed a 3-month Vipassana meditation retreat. What brought me there was my desire to know God, to know the truth behind the concept "God." I certainly learned a lot about myself in the process, and about spiritual work. But the Buddha proposed that the purpose of the path was not to find God, but to overcome suffering… and I've never suffered as much as I did in Buddhist meditation!

So rather than go to India, in the Spring of 1976 I came to Israel in search of a spiritual master who would fit what Rebbe Nahman described in another of his teachings, "The Master of the Field." How is it that rather than a Hasidic rabbi, or a master of Kabbalah, I found an Arab Muslim Sufi Sheikh? Well, that's another story...

Where we pick up our story, I'm already living in the zawiyya, the Sufi "corner" in the basement of the house of Sidi Sheikh Muhammad al Jemal. This was where Sidi's disciples or mureeds would stay, when they came to visit him on the Mount of Olives. Now I was one of them. I was practicing Islamic prayer five times a day, and I was doing my best to make inner Zikr, "remembering" God by chanting the name Allah in my heart. Within the framework of these practices, our focus as Sidi's mureeds was to understand and experience what he described as "The Stations of the Way." There were Seven Stations of the Nafs (ego) which prepared the way for the Seven Stations of the Heart, followed by Seven Stations of the Soul... culminating in the Station of al Fana(annihilation in God). And after that there were Seven further Stations of the Secret, all of which Sidi described in simple, slightly awkward, but very beautiful English. Like Sidi's other mureeds, I was copying his descriptions of these Stations, along with other teachings,into a notebook of my own. I was endeavoring to open myself to these perspectives, and I felt I was experiencing at least some of what I was writing.

After focusing on the teachings of Rebbe Nahman and other Jewish texts with Reb Zalman, it was refreshing to discover a living source of teaching. With Sidi I could see that spiritual books really come from spiritual people, and not the other way around! More than once it happened that when I asked Sidi a question, the answer he gave yielded yet another impressive teaching... which might be recorded and later transcribed.

In my own mind, I was following Islamic Sufism in much the same way as I had pursued Buddhist meditation. I respected the forms of the tradition—not as a religious identity, but as a spiritual practice. Clearly, this kind of practice suited me better than dry

Buddhist meditation. (And the more devotional practices of, say, the Tibetan Buddhist tradition, looked too much like idol-worship for me to pursue.) But while one could easily pick up Yoga or Buddhism as a spiritual interest, from a worldly perspective, Judaism and Islam were supposed to be in conflict! I was walking on the edge of the unknown… and if I felt perplexed, it was a part of the experience.

Part of becoming Sidi's disciple and "submitting to the Sheikh" so as to open oneself to God, was accepting the Arabic name that he would give. Sidi gave Arabic names to all his disciples. Well, I thought, this would be a test—for me, and maybe for him as well.

I liked my given name, Joshua. I preferred the Hebrew, Yehoshua. The simple meaning is "God will save," or to put it more concretely, "God will resolve this conflict." Like… the conflict I felt between Judaism and Islam! But I understood that the name Joshua in Arabic is 'Issa', and that Jesus in Arabic is 'Issa'. The Islamic approach to Jesus as a Prophet, rather than the Son of God, made him more approachable for me. But I wasn't sure that calling this Jewish boy from Brooklyn "Jesus" would be such a good idea!

Then, one fine morning, the day I had anticipated arrived. Sidi walked into the zawiyya, and he was smiling. Maybe he was whistling! (Do pious Muslims whistle?) He was clearly in a good mood. I could sense that he had a message for me.

"Beloved," he said (that's how he addressed his disciples), "your name is Yusuf. Yusuf is the face of the beauty. This is you. You are Yusuf."

Well, several things happened inside me at once. (Maybe some of them occurred to me later, but much of this came up immediately!) First of all, I like the name Yusuf. I like the sound of it. I don't much care for Yosef in Hebrew, or Joseph in English. That's my father's name. But the jazz musician Yusuf Latif has the most beautiful name I can imagine. Latif means the divine quality of Subtlety, and it sounds just like it. And now Sidi is calling me "Yusuf"!

As for "the face of the beauty," while it was a very nice compliment, I wasn't sure it fit. Maybe I look interesting, maybe my profile is handsome, but I never thought of myself as beautiful! This was a small consideration: a bigger one weighed on my mind.

"But Sidi," I blurted out, "that's my father's name!" I think I might have already brought my parents to meet Sidi. They moved to Israel that summer, to establish a Conservative synagogue where men and women could sit and pray together, in the holy city of Tzfat. I'm sure Sidi must have heard my father's name!

I started to ponder how intriguingly complex all of this was. On the one hand I understood that Sidi was saying, implicitly, "You are your father." Here I am sweating about my mesoret avot, my "tradition of the (male) ancestors." When Sidi spoke of "the line of the Prophets" I felt good about this—it overlapped with the Patriarchs or avotof my own Jewish heritage. (Feminists had only just begun to reconstruct "patriarchy" as a dirty word in those days, and I'm still sorry they did that. Of course, we can speak of the Matriarchs as well, but for me, the Patriarchy marks out important common ground that's shared between Judaism and Islam.) There was an English poet who said, "The son is the father of the man." I am my own father, in a sense. We contain those we've inherited from, within ourselves.

But what also occurred to me was this. Sidi often said that the Sufi Way is the Way of the Polite. Not my favorite term, "the polite." It sounds too formal and external. I was more comfortable when Sidi said, "the deep courtesy." But either way, this means seeing others as "the Face of God" and taking into consideration not only one's point of view, but respecting the forms and the beliefs in which the souls of others have wrapped themselves. In practical terms it means being gracious and considerate: being faithful to the Truth as one understands it, while doing what one can to respect the feelings of others. This wasn't the Sufism of wild and provocative dervishes that I would later find described in books like God's Unruly Friends by Ahmet Karamustafa! But if you wanted to be "polite" or considerate, well… it was totally unacceptable in the Jewish world (certainly among Ashkenazi Jews like us) for the son to take the name of his living father. If you need someone to explain, just ask Sigmund Freud!

All this was percolating in my head and in my heart. But then it also occurred to me that I didn't need to make this into a make-it-or-break-it issue. If Sidi was making a mistake—and I certainly believed that everyone, including him, could make mistakes—then maybe it's not my problem. If he's made a mistake, it's his mistake to fix. And with that thought, something in me relaxed.

Not a word had been uttered between us since I said, "That's my father's name!" There was this long pregnant pause in which I looked at Sidi, and he looked at me... and in the silence between us I felt he could hear at least some of my thoughts. Finally, he spoke:

"Knows, you are Yusuf. (I loved his imperfect English!) But maybe, better for you... your name Ya'qub."

"Sidi, that was my grandfather's name!"

"Yes, this is right. You are Yusuf... but better, your name Ya'qub."

While I thought that Sidi should have been aware of my father's name, I had no idea how he came up with my grandfather's name! It felt like divine guidance. I was more easily drawn to the sound of "Yusuf." The sound of "Ya'qub," with the guttural 'ayin and the quf in the back of the throat—which exist in Hebrew, and are emphasized in Arabic, but don't really exist in English—make it hard to pronounce. Yet I prefer the biblical character of Jacob to Joseph. I've always seen Joseph as an assimilated Egyptian government official. Whereas Jacob is a gentle Hebrew shepherd who starts out close to home, and has to learn to handle this world. He wrestles with angels and also with men, he falls in love with Rachel and then marries both Leah and Rachel... and makes a personal relationship with God, as he finds his own way in life. His example is significant. The People of Israel are named for Jacob, for the namethat he received from the angel.

So, looking back, I'm grateful to Sidi for giving me this name. Maybe Joshua, the one who first conquered the Land of Israel, got me to the Holy Land—including the Islamic Sufi dimension I found hidden in this land. Ya'qub ibn Yusuf is the Jewish Sufi who emerged.

So that was the end of that particular conversation with Sidi Sheikh Muhammad, as far as I recall. I came back to Winnipeg, Canada. And that's another story—Sidi's vision of where I was to go. Okay, it's a short story, I'll throw it in here as well. I knew that he got the "Order" and sent people wherever the Spirit showed him. Another test of our submission! My negative phantasy was that he'd send me somewhere really foreign to me... like South Africa. To make peace between the whites and blacks in that Christian land, by bringing them the true Islam! A cause that I couldn't identify with at all. (Although, years later, I had a girlfriend from South Africa—a black, Christian minister who sometimes visited Israel, and greatly admired the Jewish people.) But no, South Africa wasn't in the cards. Whew!

One day Sidi walked into the zawiyya, and again he was excited by the vision he was carrying for me:

"Beloved, there is place... special place. Like, in the middle of America. (Oh no! Oklahoma? Kansas?) Not in America... on top. With water all around. (One of the Great Lakes? Or did he mean the Red and the Assiniboine Rivers that meet in Winnipeg?) The streets there, very wide. The trees, very tall. And the people there, very polite!"

"Sidi, do you mean Winnipeg? In Canada?

"Yes... you can go to this place? Many people await you in this place."

Well, I consoled myself that my parents would be pleased— I could go back to university and complete my B.A. degree. And I had friends there, although I wasn't at all sure that people would be clamoring to get involved with the Islamic Sufism I'd be bringing back from Jerusalem. But did I share Sidi's teachings with some of my friends there, and I got involved in other kinds of other alternative activities.

After I finished my B.A., I got together with a couple of new friends who became my business partners, and we opened Prairie Sky, Winnipeg's spiritual bookstore. I was calling myself "Ya'qub" but I still hadn't done anything official about my name. And then, one day, quite out of the blue, my mild mannered partner Link Phillips (whose lady was a Jewish doctor), called me "Ya'qub Heckelman." He meant well, but I heard it immediately—it's all wrong. Giving up Joshua, or Yehoshua, while keeping the awkward Heckelman? That can't be! I had already been playing with the idea of making my last name ibn Yusuf, "son of Yusuf," since I had been given that beautiful name, Yusuf, and since it really was my father's name. Back in "the Golden Age of Muslim Spain" when Jews and Muslims got along, many Jews took Arabic names, acknowledging the names of their fathers, like ibn Gavirol, ibn Ezra, ibn Daud… (Nowadays it's more common among Arabs to make a family name based on the name of one's son, not one's father: not ibn but abu).

And then, one day, a Jewish fellow with the last name of "Edelstein" walks up to the counter at the bookstore. I ask him about his name, and it turns out that he's related to Cantor Edelstein from the synagogue we attended back in Brooklyn, who had the same last name. Actually, neither I nor my parents and my sister liked Cantor Edelstein very much. He had an impressive voice, but he felt very distant from the prayers, from God… It sounded like he was just performing, like he was listening to himself in the empty space. And then this fellow, who I think was his nephew, asks me if I knew that Cantor Edelstien was a holocaust survivor? So that's why he sounded detached from his prayers! Suddenly I felt compassion in my heart, and I forgave Cantor Edelstien for being who he was… and I asked in my heart for me and my family to be forgiven for our criticism.

So, after I get a sense of how close this fellow is to my own roots, he tells me that he's a numerologist… and into Kabbalah. In short, it seems like he's not just some secular "New Ager," he's someone who's been sent to me. So I tell him that I'm thinking of officially changing my name, and I ask him if he can give me an analysis of the implications? He writes out both names in full, within some kind of a form. And he tells me that whether it's "Josh Heckelman" or "Joshua Heckelman" (it works out the same), this fellow's a nice guy whom everyone gets along with. (Nevermind all the self-conscious jokes about my "joshing," and then "heckling" you!) But Joshua Heckelman doesn't have not much will, much power to be really creative and do something with his life. Whereas Ya'qub ibn Yusuf has a lot of creative energy to break through and accomplish things. But, as with everything in life, there's also a price to be paid. If I change my name to Ya'qub ibn Yusuf, he says, there will be people who don't like me. (He's not talking about Arabic and Islam, necessarily. This is on the basis of numerology.) Not that they'll want to kill me, but there will be some people who won't like who I am, what I stand for… who'll talk about me behind my back.

That made sense to me. And it sounded to me like price I'd be willing to pay—to get out of my head and get out into the world, and really do something creative with my life. So I went downtown, to the place on Portage Avenue where you register a change of name. I paid my $40 and I officially changed my name from Joshua Drexler Heckelman to Ya'qub ibn Yusuf.

On the Temple Mount

As I recall, the episode on the Temple Mount took place that same summer, back in 1976, when I was still getting used to living as a Sufi in Arab East Jerusalem.

Along with reflecting on Sidi's teachings, and doing Islamic prayer five times a day, our main practice in the zawiyya was Zikr Allah, literally, "Remembering the Divine," connecting with God within ourselves. We made inner Zikr by repeating the name "Allah" while focusing on the heart-center, with our eyes open or closed. I understood that I was supposed to be doing a lot of Zikr. This was the Sufi equivalent to meditation, and everything was pointing towards it. It was the thread which was meant to carry us through to the Divine. But it wasn't working for me very well at that point—

neither as a daily practice, nor on the one particular occasion when Sidi encouraged me to make a solitary "retreat" by staying up and making Zikr through the night.

That summer I heard that an older Jewish woman from Canada was coming to Jerusalem, and wanted to meet me. She had survived the holocaust as a young girl, and now she ran a modern dance studio in Toronto. But unlike the American Sufis I had met from "the Sufi Order of the West," she was a follower of the Sufi path who had embraced Islam.

I myself had mixed feelings about Islam. I appreciated salat, the daily Islamic prayers. I found it to be a very grounded practice of devotion to God. More than just praising God, or asking something of God, it was a way of gathering oneself and making oneself a vessel... opening oneself to God—standing, bowing, and in prostration, and then kneeling on the floor. But while I appreciated the prayer, I was uncomfortable with the implication that I might thereby be embracing another religion... and rejecting Judaism? I had no desire to reject my Jewish heritage. I remember going outside the zawiyya at sunset on Friday evenings and welcoming the Shabbat in my own quiet way, as I watched the changing light in the sky over the desert and the Dead Sea. Yet I wanted to pursue Islamic Sufism as a serious spiritual practice, much as I had endeavored to pursue Buddhist meditation. Sufism came more naturally to me—I was comfortable with how, in Sufi thought, a very personal sense of God connected with a broad understanding of God as the Oneness of Being —and I wanted to take it seriously. Maybe this woman would be, for me, an older sister on the path. I was looking forward to getting her perspective on what it means for a Jew to follow an Islamic-Sufi path.

She was staying at Yeshivat HaKotel and I was to meet her there. That in itself was intriguing. Why would a Jewish woman who had embraced Islam stay at "The Yeshiva by the Western Wall," which most likely was there to draw unaffiliated Jews into Orthodox Judaism? What was drawing her to Israel? Perhaps she had something to learn from me, as well, about appreciating Judaism from a Sufi perspective.

It was a clear summer day when I set out from the Mount of Olives. I didn't know exactly how to get where I was going... but since I was in no hurry, I decided to walk. My path down the hill took me by the beautiful Russian church with onion-shaped domes, and eventually I walked around from the eastern wall, to the northern wall of the Old City. I entered at the Damascus Gate.

Suddenly I was surrounded by Arab market stalls. I started heading down streets and lanes in the direction that I thought would take me to the Jewish Quarter, and then, before I knew it, I reached another gate. A friendly-looking young Israeli soldier greeted me there. I must have looked a bit confused.

"Where are you going?" he asked me. I think we may have spoken in Hebrew.

"I'm trying to get to HaKotelHaMa'aravi (the Western Wall)."

"Okay, you're close. So, do you want to go there the long way, or the short way?"

Now this was an interesting question. I wasn't sure what he meant. But Sidi Sheikh Muhammad frequently said that his was "the short way to go from the market... to the Garden of the Soul." And here was an offer to go "the short way"!

I said, "The short way."

"Okay," he said, "come right in."

I entered the gate and there I was... on the Temple Mount! I had avoided going to the Temple Mount up until this point. I knew that Sidi was some kind of official religious figure over there. But as one of his new disciples, who had little experience with what he called "the outside religion," I knew that I wasn't supposed to go there. That was fine with me. I had no desire to have to declare who I was... and possibly embarrass him, and myself. But there I was, through no effort of my own! It seemed like an opening from the universe, like an invitation from God.

Past the gate with the soldier, I didn't encounter any Arab guards waiting to question me. I found myself walking across the wide open plaza of the Temple Mount, drenched in sunlight. And there, to my left, was the golden Dome of the Rock. Well, if I had been invited, who was I to refuse? I ascended the steps. I wondered if I looked Muslim enough in my short-sleeved shirt and khaki slacks, wearing Israeli sandals and a beret on my head? Maybe I could blend in with the Muslims, as well as with the Jews. But when I got to the entrance to the mosque of the Dome, I found an Arab guard standing there.

He said, "Where's your ticket?"

"Oh, I need a ticket?"

"Yes…"

It may have been then that I first had a glimpse of the huge rough-hewn rock that's enclosed beneath the beautiful, ornate dome. But I didn't try to enter. And as I walked back down the steps, I began to reflect… they didn't say that I wasn't welcome. They said that I needed a ticket. But why did the guard assume that I wasn't a Muslim? Muslims, after all, don't buy tickets! Was it because I was wearing the wrong style sandals? Then it occurred to me that I hadn't made wudhu, the ritual washing for Islamic prayer. Maybe that was my mistake! So I headed to the washing fountain where people wash their hands, arms, face, mouth, back of the neck and feet, to prepare for prayer. I knew how to do that—I was doing it five times a day!

After I washed, I thought of going back to the Dome of the Rock. This was the rock where, according to Jewish tradition, Abraham offered his son Isaac as a sacrifice. The rock where, according to Islamic tradition, the Prophet Muhammad ascended the Seven Heavens and met the major Prophets on his way towards al Fana, annihilation in God—Prophets including Abraham, Moses, David, and Jesus and John the Baptist (some of whom we might call patriarchs, kings, or spiritual masters… but never mind). I'd already been told that I'd need a ticket to enter the Dome of the Rock, and yet I felt like I was there on the Temple Mount at God's invitation. What to do? I wasn't interested in buying a ticket. Not because of the money, but because I was there as a pilgrim. I might want to pray…

So, after washing, I decided to "play it safe" and I walked straight to the mosque on the south side of the Temple Mount: the large, rectangular Al Aqsa Mosque. I took off my shoes at the door, and entered like the other worshippers. No one seemed to notice. The room was huge. The floor was covered with all kinds of small prayer carpets, but except for some interesting carpets, there was nothing much to look at. Later I heard that there had been a fire, set by some Jewish fanatic, and whatever had been there in the way of old, wooden fixtures was destroyed in the fire.

As I was standing there at Al Aqsa, the remembrance of God, Zikr Allah, began to well-up in my heart. Wow, for once I was feeling what I was supposed to be feeling! I could really feel it, and this was now all that I wanted to do: just sit in this place and remember, "Allah… Allah!" So I sat on the carpet, closed my eyes, went inside, and began to recall "Allah" silently within myself. The one thought that came to my mind, along with making Zikr, was a line in Hebrew from Psalms: "Ahat Sha-alti…" "One thing have I asked of God. It's the same thing I'll request: to sit myself in the House of God all the days of my life, to have vision in the grace of God and to visit in His dwelling place."

I was so happy to be there! I continued my Zikr…. And then, after a little while, I felt someone approach. I opened my eyes and I saw an Arab guard. He hesitated to speak. As I recall it was me who said, "What? I can't sit down?"

He said, "Yes…"

So I stood up. I looked around. I saw that there were some tourists there, as well as a few Muslim worshippers. The tourists were looking around… at what? There was nothing to look at. I remember thinking, "There's nothing to see—outside. Someone should tell them it's all inside!"

And then it occurred to me, "This is why people are fighting over this place! There's such a presence here…" I didn't expect to find this, but at that moment I felt that a doorway to heaven, to the Presence of God, is here in this place! "So that's why everyone is fighting over this place. They all want a piece of the action. They want this access to be theirs!" I didn't have a vision of the Prophet Muhammad on his Night Journey meeting the other great Prophets, although that might have fit with what I was experiencing. I didn't think of the sacrifice of Isaac, or of Solomon's Temple. All I wanted to do was to make my own "journey" of Zikr Allah, and open myself to God… whose presence I could feel.

Then a teaching from Sidi Sheikh Muhammad came to my mind. I could hear him saying, "Not the place is holy—you are holy. Because of you, the place is holy." Wow. Up until that moment this teaching had been easy for me to accept, intellectually. Now it was challenging. It was almost impossible to understand! But I said to myself, "Don't get too attached. This place, somehow, is opening me. Wow, I really feel the opening in this place! But he's saying that I'm feeling what I'm feeling, because of what I'm bringing to this place. And yet it doesn't feel like I'm bringing anything. I feel like it's all here! So this must mean that I have to reverse the figure and the ground." I thought about the example of a lock and a key. "Am I the key, and this place is the lock? Or maybe I'm the lock, and this place is the key!" I gathered that, as impressed as I was, I shouldn't get too attached to this place. It was showing me something that somehow, I had within. And as Sidi would say, "Let's see what God makes."

As I was standing there in the mosque, what also came to mind was the way in which my teacher, Reb Zalman, had coached us about "doing spiritual work in the world." Reb Zalman would say, for example, "If you're riding on the subway, you can imagine that you're going to die at the next subway stop. And before you get to the station, you prepare yourself, summing up the whole of your life and preparing to give up everything and go back to God. And then, when you leave that station and approach the next station… you go through the same process all over again." Zalman added that if we're concerned about looking weird, we could do all this with our eyes wide open!

So rather than regretting that I couldn't sit down, close my eyes, and make a traditional Zikr, I decided to stand on my two legs with my eyes wide open and concentrate as best I could, within. I did my best to leave all further thoughts aside. Just go inside and remember: "Allah!" "Allah!" "Allah!" I wasn't doing this for very long, however, when another guard appeared. Again, I didn't wait for him to speak. I said,

"What, I can't pray?" I was standing there with my eyes wide open, but it seemed like he knew that I wasn't just looking around.

"Ye-es..." was his answer. It felt like he was reluctant to interfere with my experience, but he felt obligated to do so. I suppose I could have protested that I was making Zikr Allah, that what I was doing was Islamic. But I didn't want to go there. I didn't want to take the holiness I had touched and mix it with making claims, with any kind of argument. I didn't want to start talking about whether I was a Muslim, or a Jew, or both... or mention Sidi's name. But I bravely took another moment or two to remember God once more in my heart. And then I said to myself, "This is now within you. You carry it wherever you go." And with that I turned and I walked outside the mosque. I put on my shoes and walked into the sunlight. And I discovered that the strong sense of connection... was gone.

I don't remember the rest of the day so vividly. I guess I must have walked down the narrow path that leads from the Temple Mount to the plaza at the Western Wall, and on to YeshivatHaKotel. I don't think I found the woman I was looking for, that day—the Canadian dance director, the Muslim-Sufi Jewish holocaust survivor. But eventually I met her. And when I did, as I recall, she didn't have much empathy for "the Jewish question" I was carrying. "Why are you worried about that!?" I didn't find that she had wisdom to offer about how one's Judaism might be reconciled with Islam... and she certainly wasn't looking to learn about Judaism from me. Now it occurs to me that her issue may have been more about reconciling Islam with the secular world of modern dance!

A year or two later, I had a similar disappointment. I was still Sidi's disciple, and I stayed at the zawiyya as I did, each year, when I could make the time to come to Israel. But I was on my way for the weekend to spend a Shabbat with my parents at their Conservative synagogue in Tzfat. And I decided to stop in Haifa on the way, and meet the "notorious"Brother Daniel. Somehow I had managed to contact the famous Christian monk, who as a Jewish boy had been saved from the holocaust by the brothers in a Christian monastery. He later chose to convert to Christianity and became a monk himself. Although Brother Daniel had come to Israel as a Christian monk, once he was here he tried to make 'aliya and become an Israeli citizen—insisting that he was Jewish according to "the law of return." His was a controversial legal case. I remember my father saying that although he was allowed to live in Israel, Brother Daniel was not accepted as an Israeli citizen according to Israeli law. But technically, my father said, according to Jewish law, he should have been accepted. There is the Rabbinic dictum, "Israel, although she has sinned, is still Israel." (That is, "Even if a Jew betrays his People and their God, he remains Jewish.") Maybe my father was trying to gently communicate something about this to me…

I can remember sitting with Brother Daniel in his room on a dark and chilly Thursday evening, and asking him about his connection to Judaism. He said that his accepting Jesus as the Messiah didn't conflict with his being Jewish. That seemed a bit cerebral to me. I asked, didn't he miss the Shabbat? (For me it's my love of the Sabbath, first of all, which has kept me Jewish.) Brother Daniel's response came to me as a shock. He proceeded to talk like a secular academic scholar, about how the prohibitions of the Sabbath were based on pagan superstitions in which Saturday is regarded as sacred to the god Saturn. People believed that if you work on Saturday, it'll bring you bad luck. They got attached to this idea, and it was later transferred to Judaism.

What? Even if this were true, had he no idea about the joy and the peace and the presence of God that one can feel on Shabbat?And the sense of joining with all of the people, in the present and the past, who share this sense of Shabbat? Surely it's something positive, whether one chooses to practice it or not. It's not a pagan superstition about avoiding bad luck! I'm not sure how much of this

I was able to articulate to him at the time. But I didn't find much common ground with Brother Daniel, even if we were both hyphenated Jews.

Looking back I can see that although I made a public statement by adopting an Arabic name, I understood that neither my Jewish parents nor my Muslim sheikh would want me to become a controversial figure like Brother Daniel. Over the course of the seven years that I followed Sidi, I kept the Fast of Ramadan, and I tried to make the Islamic prayers five times a day, six days a week. But on Shabbat I made the Jewish prayers, and I observed the Jewish holidays as well. And I felt that all this time Sidi was waiting for me to fully embrace Islam... but that it didn't fit for me. This was very frustrating for me, and eventually I asked him to release me. Very soon I found myself a new spiritual home in the world of Turkish Sufism. There I haven't felt pressure to become more Islamic, although I've sometimes felt like I'll never quite be "secular" enough to meet people's expectations! But I've come to understand that the spiritual bridges we need to build—they're not just between Judaism and Islam. Living in Israel has shown me how important it is to build bridges between the poles of the "secular" and the "religious," so that people will feel free to integrate what's meaningful for them.

It was seven years after I let go of Sidi that I came back to Israel to study Kabbalah at the Hebrew University in Jerusalem. I stayed, and I made 'aliya as a Jew with a classical Arabic name. It was seven year later, in 1997, that I opened the spiritual bookstore Olam Qatan, where I've published in Hebrew some books of Sufi poetry and a book of Kabbalah, and where I recently put together and published, in English, Dervish Yunus Emre: the Turkish Sufi Poet who came after Rumi.

Looking back, I'm grateful for the brief but profound experience that I was granted on the Temple Mount—and for the grace which allowed me to move in and out of that experience, without making a big fuss. Although I've been back to the Temple Mount since then, several times, nothing has happened which approaches what I experienced that first time. So be it. Now, as I look back, I'm grateful to be able to share the story of what happened.

About Raheel Raza

Raheel Raza is President of The Council for Muslims Facing Tomorrow, founding member of The Muslim Reform Movement, Director of Forum for Learning, award winning journalist, public speaker, advocate for human rights, gender equality and dignity in diversity.

VISION AND GOALS

- EXPOSE the dangers of a radical Islamist ideology and take back the faith.
- EMPOWER women for rights and gender equality.
- EDUCATE youth about the dangers of radicalization and terrorism.

MEDIA

- Raheel has appeared in print and on TV and radio numerous times including CNN, Real Time with Bill Maher, BBC Hardtalk, CBC, CTV, TVO, Tucker Carlson.
- In 2017 she gave over 250 interviews internationally and published over a dozen op-eds.
- WTN (Women's Television Network) featured Raheel in their special documentary series titled "Family Dance".

HUMAN RIGHTS

- In her pursuit for human rights, Raheel is accredited with the United Nations Human Rights Council in Geneva through The Centre for Inquiry (CFI). She attends sessions thrice a year.

Awards

- Recipient of Canada's Sesquicentennial commemorative medal for 'exceptional contributions to Canada'.
- Recipient of the Queen Elizabeth II Diamond Jubilee medal for service to Canada.
- City of Toronto's Constance Hamilton award
- The Urban Hero award
- Participant in the award winning documentary "Honor Diaries"
- First Pakistani woman to be included in Canada Heirloom series titled "Millennium"

Speaking Engagements

- Universities across USA including Harvard, Columbia and Brandeis
- UK at Oxford and Cambridge
- Parliaments of Sweden, UK, Israel and Capitol Hill in Washington DC
- Tedx Amsterdam
- School Boards and Places of worship
- The Israeli Presidential Conference in Jerusalem
- Training sessions for law enforcement in Mesa, AZ for Maricopa County Sheriff's Department

ACHIEVEMENTS

- In July 2017 Raheel gave testimony to the US Congress on "Combating Homegrown Terrorism"
- She runs a Forum for Learning with panels, discussions and international speakers
- She has taught courses on various aspects of Islam at George Brown College and Ryerson University in Toronto for the past five years
- Raheel has made a documentary film called "Whose Sharia is it anyway?" dealing with the sharia debate in Ontario, Canada.
- Testified before the Canadian Parliament on Bill S-7, which became the Zero Tolerance of Barbaric Cultural Practices Act.

BOARDS

- Advisory Board of The Clarion Project
- Executive Advisory Board of The Mackenzie Institute,
- Advisory Board of The ACTV Foundation (The Alliance of Canadian Terror Victims).
- Munk Senior Fellow with The Macdonald-Laurier Institute
- Board member for Creative Cultural Communications
- Steering Committee of Parliament of World Religions

PUBLICATIONS

Their Jihad–Not My Jihad, Basileia Books, 2005

Their Jihad–Not My Jihad 3rd Edition, Possibly Publishing, 2014

How Can You Possibly be a Muslim Feminist?, Possibly Publishing, 2014

Paper: *The Rise of Islamic Extremism in Canada*, Mackenzie Institute, 2013

Journeys of a Spiritual Activist, Possibly Publishing, 2017

CONTACT INFORMTAION

info@raheelraza.com

416-505-6052

www.muslimsfacingtomorrow.com

www.honordiaries.com/tedx/raheel-raza-tedxwomen-amsterdam

www.muslimreformmovement.org

www.ingramcontent.com/pod-product-compliance
Lightning Source LLC
LaVergne TN
LVHW010018070426
835512LV00001B/9

9780615792170